DATE DUE

DEMCO 38-297

Books adapted and edited by
Robert Meredith and E. Brooks Smith
PILGRIM COURAGE
THE COMING OF THE PILGRIMS
RIDING WITH CORONADO
THE QUEST OF COLUMBUS

The Quest of Columbus

C·C· 1492

THE QUEST OF COLUMBUS

A Detailed and Exact Account of the Discovery
Of America with the Many Difficulties, Dangers,
And Triumphant Return

*Being the History Written
By Ferdinand Columbus,
Son of Christopher Columbus,
Admiral of the Ocean Sea,
Who, as a Boy of Thirteen,
Sailed with His Father on the Fourth Voyage
And Heard the Story of the First*

Edited and Adapted
By Robert Meredith and E. Brooks Smith
From *The History of the Life and Actions of
Admiral Christopher Colon* by Ferdinand Colon,
The First English Translation, Prepared for
Churchill's *Voyages* (1744-1746)
And Including the Letter of Columbus
To Luis Santángel Reporting His Discovery

*Illustrated
by Leonard Everett Fisher*

BOSTON   Little, Brown and Company   TORONTO

To those, of all ages, who dream the truth
and dare to make their dreams come true

Foreword

COLUMBUS charted a course where no man hitherto had dared, and with torches flaring as a signal to keep his little fleet together, sailed into the western night. Some men content themselves with retracing old routes and think that seeking new ways is a waste of time. They get to know the old routes better by limiting their number and travel them as a habit, without thought. They feel threatened by new ways and even deny the possibility of their existence. But there are always a few men who, although they know the old ways well, leave their minds open to new and better ones — or the one that will take them off the map and into a new world. When they are told, "You can't get there from here," they reserve the right to try. He who would discover must first admit that discovery is possible, and welcome discoveries when they come knocking at his door. Then he must have the courage to brave the unknown as well as fight the fears and doubts of his fellow men. At last he parts the curtains of darkness and looks upon the sleeping face of Knowledge.

Some men then and now would say, "Stay home and solve the problems of the Old World before finding a new." Today we hear, "Let us look deeper into the earth before reaching for the moon," or "We run away from the problems of the world when we go out into space."

They set up opposing poles and say you must choose one
or the other, discover this and not that. But the spirit of
discovery is indivisible. Discoverers map the heart of man
as well as Hispaniola, they seek the center of the earth as
well as Mars, they cross the Atlantic or probe the Pacific
depths, but the most important journey must first be made
in the mind. And only free spirits go on such quests.

When Columbus sailed into the unknown, he brought
light to the mind of man as well as illuminating the dark
side of the globe. He helped to break the bonds of ignorance and inertia that held man back, and gave him a
new birth. What the Old World did with the New and
what man did with his new freedom are another story, but
the whole tale is not yet told, and the light Columbus lit
shines still, and hearts are high with hope that further discoveries will bring mankind closer to the happiness the
Admiral did not find in America, except in the act of discovery itself.

Main Historical Persons of the Narrative

Christopher Columbus, Admiral of the Ocean Sea

Ferdinand Columbus, second son of the Admiral and author of this account

Diego Columbus, first son of the Admiral

Bartholomew Columbus, brother of the Admiral

Ferdinand and *Isabella,* called the Catholic Sovereigns, King and Queen of Spain

Fray Juan Pérez, a friar, head of the monastery of La Rábida near Palos, Spain, and friend to the Admiral

Luis de Santángel, secretary of treasury in the Spanish royal household and promoter of the Admiral's cause

Martín Alonso Pinzón, captain of the caravel *Pinta*

Vincent Yañez Pinzón, brother of Martín Alonso and captain of the caravel *Niña*

Guacanagarí, cacique or chieftain in the Indies, the Admiral's friend

John II, King of Portugal

Portuguese governor of the island of Santa Maria in the Azores

Contents

Contents

Contents

The Quest of Columbus

Ferdinand Columbus to the Reader

I, BEING the son of the Admiral Christopher Columbus who discovered America and is worthy of eternal memory, having sailed with him for some time, it seemed reasonable to me that among the things I have written, one, and the main one, should be his life and wonderful discovery of the New World.

His hardships and later sickness did not allow him time to turn his notes and observations into a history. Yet knowing many others had tried this work, I held back, until I read their books. I found they make large of some things, make little of others, and sometimes pass over in silence what they ought to tell in full.

For this reason I decided to undergo the labor of this task, thinking it better that I should be blamed for trying more than I could do and lack of skill than to allow the truth of what relates to so noble a person to lie buried. It is my comfort that if any fault be found in my undertaking, it will not be that which most historians have — not knowing the truth of what they write.

I promise to make the history of my father's life out of such matter as I find in his own papers and letters, of those events of which I was an eyewitness, and no other. And whoever thinks that I add anything of my own to the telling, may be sure that I cannot hope to profit in this life or the life to come by stretching the truth. The reader alone will profit from this history if it yield any.

[Columbus says of the conduct of the thirteen-year-old Ferdinand on the difficult fourth voyage in a letter to the king: "Our Lord gave him such courage that he revived the spirit of the others, and he acted as if he had been a sailor of eighty years, and he consoled me."]

I

Of the Admiral's Person, and What Sciences He Learned

THE ADMIRAL was well-built and taller than average, his body neither fat nor lean. His face was long, with a hawk nose, light-colored eyes, and high cheekbones. His complexion was light and tended toward bright red. In youth his hair had been red, but when he reached thirty years of age, it all turned gray. In his eating, drinking, and dress he was always modest and sparing. Among strangers his manner was courteous and friendly. With members of his household he was pleasant, although grave and dignified. He was so strict in matters of religion that for all his fasting and praying he might be thought a member of some religious order. He was so much an enemy of swearing and cursing that I never heard him say anything worse than "by St. Ferdinand." When he was most angry at anybody, he would say, "God take you" for doing or saying that. When he had something to write, he tried out his pen with the words, "Jesus and Mary be with us on our course." He wrote with such a fine hand he might have earned his bread by it.

Bypassing other details of his personal traits and manners which will be brought up at the proper time in this history, let us speak of what sciences he devoted himself to. He learned his letters at a tender age and studied the geographers, of whose works he was fond. He was also fond of astronomy and geometry, sciences so closely related that one cannot do without the other. Because Ptolemy in the beginning of his geography says that no man can be a good geographer unless he knows how to draw, the Admiral learned to draw in order to show the position of lands and set down geographic bodies, plane and round.

II

What the Admiral Did Before He Came to Spain

HAVING gained knowledge in these sciences, the Admiral went to sea and made voyages to the east and west. Of these voyages and many other things of his early days, I have no perfect knowledge, because he died while I was still young and not so bold as to ask him about his youth. To tell the truth, being just a boy, I was not troubled by such matters. But in a letter to Their Catholic Majesties in 1501, to whom he dare not write anything but the truth, he wrote these words:

Most Serene Princes:

I went to sea very young and followed it to this day. The art of sailing makes those who practice it want to discover the secrets of the earth. For more than forty years I have been sailing to all parts of the known world. I have dealt and spoken with wise men, both clergy and lay, Latins, Greeks, Jews, Moors, and many others.

I found Our Lord most favorable to my desire to know the secrets of the earth, and He has given me the gift of understanding. He has made me skillful in navigation and supplied me well with astronomy, geometry, and arithmetic. God has given me a genius and hands suited to draw this globe, and on it the cities, rivers, mountains, islands, and ports, each in its proper place. During this time I have tried to read all the books written on geography, history, philosophy, and other sciences.

Thus Our Lord made it known to me that I might sail from here to the Indies, and gave me the burning desire to do so. Filled with this desire, I came to Your Highnesses. All who heard of my undertaking, rejected it with contempt and scorn. They paid no heed to the arguments I gave or the authorities I cited. Only Your Highnesses had faith and confidence in me.

In another letter, written from Hispaniola in January, 1495, to Their Catholic Majesties, telling them of the errors and variations commonly found in pilots' sailing directions and other charts, he says:

It happened to me that King René (whom God has taken) sent me to Tunis to take the galleass *Fernandina*. When I was off the island of San Pietro near Sardinia, I was told there were two ships and a carrack with the galleass, which frightened my men. They resolved to go no farther, but to return to Marseilles for another ship and more men. I, seeing that I could not go against their will, without some ruse, yielded to their desires. Changing the point of the compass needle, I set sail at nightfall, and next morning at daybreak we found ourselves off Cape Cathage. All aboard thought we had been sailing for Marseilles.

In the same manner is a piece he wrote to prove the five zones are navigable, using the experiences of his voyage as proof. He says:

In February, 1467, I sailed a hundred leagues beyond Iceland, whose northern part is seventy-three degrees north, and not sixty-three as some claim. To this island, which is big as England, the English come to trade, especially from Bristol. At the time I was there, the sea was not frozen, but the tides were so great that in some places it rose twenty-six fathoms and fell as many.

Then seeking to prove the Equator is habitable, he says, "I was in the fort of St. George de la Mina belonging to the King of Portugal, and below the Equator, and I am a witness that it is not uninhabitable, as some say."

And in the book of his first voyage, he says he saw some mermaids on the coast of Malagueta [Liberia], but they did not look as much like ladies as had been reported. Elsewhere he says, "In sailing from Lisbon to Guinea I found by making careful calculations many times that a degree on the earth is fifty-six and two-thirds terrestrial miles." In another place he says, "I followed the sea twenty-three years without being off it any time worth speaking of. I saw all the east and all the west (including England) and have been to Guinea, yet I have never seen harbors as good as those of the West Indies." A little farther on he says that he took to the sea at fourteen and followed it ever after.

In the book of the second voyage he says, "I had two ships and left one in Porto Santo for a day for repairs, yet I got to Lisbon eight days before the other because

I had a favorable gale from the southwest and she had light contrary winds from the northeast."

From the examples we may gather how much experience he had in sailing and how many lands and places he visited before he undertook his discovery.

III

Of the Admiral's Coming to Portugal and What Happened to Him There Which Was the Cause of His Discovery of the Indies

THE ADMIRAL sailed with a fleet from Genoa going to England and Flanders with cargo in time of war. The fleet was attacked by a French and Portuguese fleet near Cape St. Vincent, Portugal. The ships grappled and began to fight furiously. They boarded each other and moved back and forth from vessel to vessel, using firepots as well as their weapons. After they had fought from morning to night, many were killed on both sides. The Admiral's ship took fire and so did the great galley it was grappled to by iron hooks and chains, which seafaring men use for that purpose. Because of the confusion and fright of the fire, the ships could not be separated.

The fire spread so fast there was nothing to do but leap into the water and drown rather than face the torture of burning.

But the Admiral, being an excellent swimmer, and seeing himself not much more than two leagues from shore, caught an oar which good fortune offered him and headed there. Sometimes swimming and sometimes resting on the oar, it pleased God, who preserved him for greater ends, to give him strength to reach land. Tired and spent with being in the water, he could hardly pull himself ashore.

He was not far from Lisbon where he knew there were some of his Genoese countrymen, so he went there as fast as he could. He made himself known to them and was so courteously received and entertained, that he set up house in that city. Because he behaved himself honorably, was a handsome man, and did nothing but what was just, it happened that a lady whose name was Doña Felipa Perestrello, of a good family, who lived and studied at the Convent of All Saints, where the Admiral went to Mass, was so taken with him that she became his wife.

His father-in-law, Bartholomew Perestrello, was dead, so they went to live with his mother-in-law. She, seeing he was so interested in geography, told him her husband had been a great seafaring man, and that he with two other captains got the King of Portugal's permission to make discoveries and divide what they found. Being thus agreed, they sailed away to the southwest and reached the islands of Madeira and Porto Santo, places never before discovered. The Admiral's father-in-law governed Porto Santo until he died.

Seeing the Admiral much delighted in hearing such voyages and relations, his mother-in-law gave him journals and sea charts left her by her husband, which inflamed the Admiral even more. He asked about other voyages the Portuguese then made to St. George de la Mina and along the coast of Guinea, being much pleased to talk to those who had been there. To say the truth, I cannot ce ainly tell, while this wife lived, whether the Admiral went to Mina or Guinea, but it seems likely.

As one thing leads to another and one thought to another, while he was in Portugal he began to think that as the Portuguese travelled so far southward, why not sail westward? Land might be found in that direction. That he might be more certain and confident, he began to look over all the geographers again, whom he had read before, and to see how astronomy might support this project. He took notice of what anybody, especially sailors, said on this subject which might help in any way. He made such good use of these things that he concluded for certain that there were many lands west of the Canary Islands and Cape Verde, and that it was possible to sail and discover them. But to make it clear how the Admiral came to build so great a house as America on such small foundations and to satisfy many who want to know the exact reasons that caused him to believe there was land to the west and dare to seek it, I will set down here what I have found in his papers on this subject.

IV

The Admiral's Reasons for Thinking He Could Sail to the Indies

I SHALL now give the three things that caused the Admiral to try to discover the Indies: natural reason, geographical writings, and the reports of sailors. By natural reason he concluded that the land and the sea made up a sphere or globe. By going from east to west and travelling around it, a man would come back to the place he started.

He held it to be true, and was supported by many learned writers, that a great part of the globe had already been travelled over, and that only a little part was left to complete the circle, that part from the eastern bounds of India, known to Ptolemy, eastward to the Azores and Cape Verde Islands. He concluded that the space between India and the Cape Verde Islands could not be more than a third part of the circumference of the globe. If such space were water, it might easily be sailed in a few days. If it were land, it could best be discovered by sailing west. The geographers made him think the globe was small, and as the eastern borders of India were unknown, those borders must lie close to the west of Spain and might properly be called Indies.

Some blamed the Admiral later for calling them Indies because they were not. The Admiral did not call them that because they had been seen and named by another, but as an eastern part of India beyond the Ganges which was unknown and had no other name. He gave them the name of what he thought was the nearest country, calling them West Indies. Also he knew all men were aware of the riches and wealth of the Indies. He thought to tempt the King and Queen of Spain by saying he went to discover the Indies by way of the west.

The support of learned authorities caused the Admiral to believe he was right. Master Paolo [Paolo dal Pozzo Toscanelli], a physician of Florence, encouraged him to make the voyage. The Admiral wrote to him, sending him a small globe and his plan. Master Paolo wrote the Admiral as follows:

To Christopher Columbus, Paolo the physician wishes health.

I received your letters with the things you sent me, which I take as a great favor, and commend your noble and ardent desire to sail from east to west, as it is marked on the chart I sent you, which would be better shown on a globe. I am glad it is well understood, and that the voyage marked out is not only possible, but true, certain, honorable, very advantageous, and most glorious among all Christians.

When this voyage is made, it will be to powerful kingdoms, to most noble cities and provinces, rich and abounding in all things we stand in need of, particularly in all sorts of spices in great quantities and great store of jewels. The kings and princes there, who are very eager to talk and trade with our countries, either to become Christians or communicate with our wise men in religion and science because of the unusual things they hear of the kingdoms of these parts, will be most grateful.

For these reasons and many others, I do not wonder that you, who have a great heart, and the Portuguese nation which has always had notable men in all undertakings, are eager to make this voyage.

This letter encouraged the Admiral very much to go on his voyage of discovery, although what the doctor earlier wrote about the first land they should meet would be Cathay and the empire of the Great Khan was false, as experience has shown that the distance from our Indies to Cathay, is greater than from here to our Indies.

V

How the Admiral Grew Angry with the King of Portugal After Offering to Discover the Indies for Him

THE ADMIRAL now concluded that his opinion was well-grounded and made up his mind to put it in practice. He would sail west in quest of those countries. Knowing that the undertaking would need the backing of a prince, he decided to go to the King of Portugal because he lived in his country.

King John gave ear to the Admiral's proposals, but he seemed slow in doing anything about them because of the great trouble and expense of the exploration and conquest of the western coast of Africa, called Guinea. He had no great success there and had not gone around the Cape of Good Hope yet. For these reasons, he had little intention of laying out more money for discoveries.

However, he listened to the Admiral because of his excellent reasons for wanting to sail west. All that was left to do was to make terms with the Admiral. Being a man of noble and generous spirit, the Admiral wanted to make an agreement that would benefit and honor him. He hoped he might leave a name and a family after his death, as a man of great actions and merits should.

To keep from having to pay a great reward, the King, by the advice of a Doctor Calzadilla, decided to send a ship secretly to try what the Admiral proposed. He speedily equipped a caravel and sent it to Cape Verde Islands, where it was to go the way the Admiral had told the King. But those the King sent lacked the knowledge, determination, and spirit of the Admiral. After wandering many days at sea, they turned back to the Cape Verdes, laughing at the undertaking and saying it was impossible there should be land in the seas. This came to the Admiral's ear, and his wife being now dead, he took a dislike to Lisbon and Portugal, and decided to go to Spain with his little son.

Fearing the King of Spain might not agree to his proposal, the Admiral sent his brother Bartholomew to England. While on his way there, he fell into the hands of pirates who took everything he had. He came to England sick and poor, so it was a long time before he could deliver his message. He made sea charts to restore his losses, and then made some proposals to King Henry VII, who then reigned. He presented a map of the world to the King, which I find among the Admiral's papers, with the following written on it:

> Whoever desires to know the coasts of countries must be taught by this map what Strabo, Ptolemy, and Isidorus say, although they do not agree in all points. Made by Bartholomew Columbus, of the red earth, a Genoese, published in London, February 21, 1480.
> Praise God.

The King of England, having seen the map and what the Admiral offered to do, readily accepted it and ordered him to be sent for. But God had saved the discovery for Spain, where the Admiral had gone and met with success, as will be shown.

VI

The Admiral's Departure from Portugal and His Talks with Their Catholic Majesties, King Ferdinand and Queen Isabella

I SHALL now leave telling how Bartholomew Columbus went to England and return to the Admiral. About the year 1484, he stole away from Portugal with his son Diego for fear of being stopped by the King. The King, knowing he had sent men of poor quality with the caravel, was of a mind to restore the Admiral to his favor. He was not as fast in carrying out this plan as the Admiral was in getting away, so he lost his chance. The Admiral got to Spain to try his fortune, which was to favor him.

He left his son at a monastery in Palos called La Rábida and went to the Spanish Court, which was then at Córdoba. Being friendly and a pleasant talker, he made friends with such men as he found interested in his idea and most likely to persuade the King to undertake it. Among them was Luis de Santángel, a man of great intelligence and influence.

As the matter required learning rather than empty words and special favor, the King and Queen turned it over to the Prior of Prado and some geographers to consider it fully and make a report. There were few geographers then, so the ones called together were not as skillful as they should have been. Also, the Admiral did not want to tell too much, for fear he might be treated as he was in Portugal, and cheated of his reward.

The reports they gave Their Highnesses differed greatly. Some said that since so many thousand years had passed since creation and so many skillful sailors had got no knowledge of such countries, it was not likely the Admiral would know more than all the men who had ever lived or then lived.

Others used geographical reasons. They said the world was so large that it was hard to believe that even three years' sail would bring him to the Far East, where he meant to sail. To support what they said they cited Seneca, who in one of his works said wise men disagreed about whether the ocean was boundless or not, and whether lands would be found on the other side or not.

Others argued as the Portuguese had about sailing to Guinea, saying that if any man sailed west, he would not be able to return to Spain because of the roundness of the globe. They looked on it as most certain that whosoever left the hemisphere known to Ptolemy would go down, as if down a hill, and would not be able to sail back without the stiffest wind.

The Admiral answered all these objections well enough. But the more powerful his reasons were, the less they understood because of their ignorance. When a man has had wrong ideas in mathematics for a long time, he cannot see the true because of the false notions first imprinted in his mind. In short, all of them held to the Spanish proverb, "St. Augustine questions it," even though it is contrary to reason. St. Augustine said it was impossible that there should be an opposite side of the earth or any going out of one hemisphere into another.

They gave judgment against the enterprise as vain and not possible, and said that it did not fit the state and dignity of great princes to be moved by such weak information. After much time spent on the subject, Their Highnesses answered the Admiral that they were busy with wars and conquests, particularly the conquest of Granada, the last Moorish stronghold in Spain, and therefore could not give their attention to the new undertaking. Later they could more conveniently examine and carry out what he proposed. To conclude, Their Majesties would not seriously give ear to the great proposals he made.

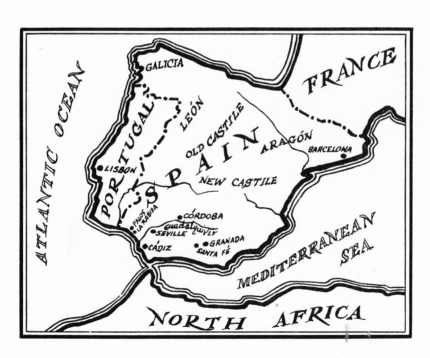

VII

How the Admiral, Not Reaching an Agreement with Their Catholic Majesties, Decided to Offer His Services Elsewhere

WHILE all of this was going on, Their Catholic Majesties had not stayed in one place because of the war in Granada. For this reason, it took them a long time to make up their minds and give an answer. The Admiral went to Seville, where he found them no more resolved than at first. He gave the Duke of Medina Sidonia an account of his project. After many conferences, he felt there was no likelihood of their support and that his plan was delayed too much. He decided to take his plan to the King of France, to whom he had already written. If he could get no hearing in France, he would go next to England to seek his brother, of whom he had no news.

Having made up his mind, he set out for the monastery of La Rábida to get his son Diego, whom he had left there, and send him to Córdoba, then go to France. But so that the end God had decreed should come about, He put it in the heart of Fray Juan Pérez, who was head of La Rábida, to become a close friend of the Admiral and be so taken with the project that he feared Spain would suffer great loss if the Admiral should leave. He begged him not to go, for he would go to the Queen, and as he was her father confessor, she might listen to what he had to say to her.

Though the Admiral was no longer hopeful and was disgusted to see so little resolution and judgment in the advisors of Their Highnesses, on the other hand, he wanted Spain to benefit from the undertaking, so he did what the friar asked. He now looked upon himself as a Spaniard as he had been there so long pursuing his project and because he had children there. He rejected offers made by other princes, writing to the King and Queen of Spain, "So I might serve Your Highnesses, I have refused to consider with France, England, and Portugal the matter of their letters which Your Highnesses may see in the hands of Doctor Villalón."

VIII

How the Admiral Returned to the Camp Before Granada and Took Leave of Their Catholic Majesties

THE ADMIRAL left La Rábida with Fray Juan Pérez for the camp of Santa Fé where Their Catholic Majesties then were, carrying on the siege of Granada.

Fray Juan told the Queen more and pressed the matter so that it pleased Her Majesty to renew the conferences about the voyage of discovery. On one side the Prior of Prado and his followers did not agree as to whether the voyage was possible or not. Columbus on the other asked to be made admiral and viceroy, as well as getting a large share of any profits. He asked too much to be granted to him if what he promised succeeded, and in case it did not, they thought it folly to give such great titles. All of this made the business come to nothing.

I cannot help saying that I consider highly the Admiral's wisdom, resolution, and foresight. He had been unfortunate in this affair and had an earnest desire to stay in Spain, and was so in need that he ought to have taken any terms. But a greatness of spirit caused him not to accept anything but great titles and honors. He could not have made better or more honorable terms if he had foreseen the success of the project. At last they were forced to grant that he should be Admiral of the Ocean Sea, and enjoy all the titles, privileges, and powers that the Admirals of Castile and León had in their several seas; government and administration of justice in all the islands and continents discovered should be entirely his. As for profit and revenues, he demanded, over and above his salary and rights as admiral, viceroy, and governor, one-tenth of all that was bought, bartered, found, or got within the bounds of his admiralship — allowing for the cost of conquest to be taken out. If one thousand ducats were found on an island, he would get one hundred.

As his opponents said he put nothing in the undertaking, but had the command of a fleet for nothing, he asked one-eighth of what the fleet brought home and offered to

pay one-eighth of the cost of the fleet. He asked so much
that Their Highnesses refused to grant it. The Admiral
took leave of his friends and went toward Córdoba, with
plans to go to France. He had made up his mind not to
go to Portugal again, although the King had written asking him to.

IX

Their Catholic Majesties Send After the Admiral and Grant Him All He Asks

IT WAS the month of January, 1492 when the Admiral
left the camp of Santa Fé. That same day, Luis de Santángel, mentioned before, who did not approve his going
and tried to stop him, went to Queen Isabella. He used
such words as he could command to persuade her and
take her to task at the same time. He said he was surprised to see Her Highness, who always had a great soul
for all matters of importance, lacking the heart to ven-
ture upon an undertaking where so little was risked and
so much to be gained. The voyage would be for the glory
of God and the spread of the faith, and not without great
benefit and honor to her kingdoms. In short, if any other
prince should undertake it, as the Admiral offered, the

damage to her crown would be easy to see. She would be much blamed with just cause by her friends and servants, not to mention her enemies. All would say she deserved the misfortune. And even if she did not have cause to repent, her heirs would feel the pain of it.

Therefore, since the matter seemed to be grounded on reason, and the Admiral who proposed it a man of sense and wisdom, and demanded no other reward than what he should find, being willing to share the cost as well as risk his life, Her Highness ought not to look upon it as such an impossibility as those scholars made it. What they said about its being a reflection on her if the enterprise did not succeed was folly, and he was of a contrary opinion, rather believing she would be looked on as generous and great-spirited for attempting to discover the secrets and wonders of the world, as other monarchs had done and been praised for.

Even though the outcome was uncertain, a large sum of money would be well used in clearing such doubt. Besides the Admiral only asked 2,500 escudos to fit the fleet, and she ought not to turn down the proposal or it would be said the fear of spending so small a sum kept her back.

The Queen, knowing the sincerity of Santángel's words, answered, thanking him for his good advice and saying she was willing to accept the proposal if it were put off until she had time to catch her breath after the war just finished. Yet if he were against waiting, she would favor borrowing money on her jewels to fit out the fleet.

Santángel, seeing she had, on his advice, agreed to what she had refused to all others, replied that there was no need of pawning her jewels. He would do her the small service of lending her the money. Having made up her mind, the Queen immediately sent an officer to bring the Admiral back. He was overtaken on the bridge of Pinos, two leagues from Granada.

The Admiral was much concerned at the difficulties and delays he had met with on this enterprise, yet learning the Queen's will and resolution, he returned to the camp at Santa Fé, where he was well entertained by Their Catholic Majesties. Their secretary, Juan de Coloma, at their command prepared a document and under their seal and signatures gave him all that he had asked for without changing a thing.

X

How the Admiral Fitted Out Three Vessels to Go on His Voyage of Discovery

WITH his terms agreed to by Their Majesties, he set out from Granada on May 12, 1492 for Palos, the port where he was to fit out his ships. The town owed Their Highnesses three months' service with two caravels, which they ordered should be given to the Admiral. These two and another he fitted out with all care and diligence. The ship he went in was called the *Santa María,* another was *La Pinta,* of which Martín Alonso Pinzón was captain, and a caravel with square sails, *La Niña,* of which Martín Alonso's brother, Vincent Yañez was captain. These brothers were from Palos.

Furnished with everything necessary and ninety men, they set sail for the Canary Islands on the third of August. From that time on, the Admiral was very careful to keep an exact journal of all that happened on the voyage, telling what wind blew, how far he sailed with every wind, what currents he found, and what he saw on the way, whether birds, fishes or other things. He did this on all four voyages he made from Spain to the Indies. I will not write of all those particulars. Though an account of the voyage, with all the differences between the sea and

land there and here in Spain might be beneficial, I think too many details might tire the reader. I will only tell what is necessary and fitting.

XI

How the Admiral Reached the Canary Islands and Took Aboard All He Needed

THE DAY after leaving for the Canary Islands, Saturday the fourth of August, the rudder of the caravel *La Pinta* broke loose. She was forced to take in her sails. The Admiral soon came to her side, but the wind blew so hard he could give no help. Yet commanders at sea have to stand by to encourage those in distress. The Admiral stayed also because he thought the master might have caused the accident so he would not have to go on the voyage. He had tried to get out of it before they sailed. Pinzón was an able seaman, so he soon fixed the rudder with the help of some ropes and was able to continue. On the Tuesday following, the weather was rough and the ropes broke. The fleet had to lay to again to mend what had given way. A suspicious person might have foreseen future disobedience to the Admiral, when through the malice of Pinzón, *La Pinta* left the fleet twice as will be told later.

They applied the best remedy they could for the present so they could get to the Canaries, which all three ships saw on the ninth of August about daybreak. But the wind was against them and they could not come to anchor at Grand Canary, either that day or the day following, though they were very near it. Here the Admiral left Pinzón and went ashore to try to get another ship. He went to the island Gomera with the *Santa María* and *La Niña* to see if he could find a vessel there, in case Pinzón could not get one on Grand Canary.

He got to Gomera on the twelfth of August and sent his boat ashore, which returned in the morning with news that there was not a vessel on the island at that time. But Doña Beatriz de Bobadilla, mistress of the island, was then at Grand Canary and had hired a vessel of forty tons which was fit for the voyage and might be had. The Admiral decided to wait there for Pinzón, believing that if Pinzón could not repair the vessel, he could get another on Gomera. He waited two days, but the vessel did not come. He sent a man on a brig bound for Grand Canary to tell Pinzón where the *Santa María* lay and help him fix his rudder, writing that he did not come himself because the *Santa María* was a poor sailer. Not receiving an answer, after many days, he decided on the twenty-third of August to return with his two vessels to Grand Canary. Sailing the next day, he overtook the brig, which still had not reached Grand Canary because of contrary winds.

Taking off the man he had sent aboard the brig, he sailed that night by Tenerife, where they saw flames gush out of the high volcano. As the men wondered at it, he told them what caused it, and compared it to Mount Etna in Sicily and other volcanoes. Passing that island, they reached Grand Canary on Saturday the twenty-fifth, which Pinzón has just reached the day before, with much difficulty.

Pinzón told him that Doña Beatriz had sailed the Monday before with the ship he was trying so hard to get. The rest being much troubled at it, he made the best of what happened. He said that since it did not please God he should see the vessel, it was perhaps because he would meet some difficulty in taking it over, and lose time in loading and unloading cargo, which would have hindered the voyage. He feared that if he went to Gomera again, he might miss it on the way. He decided to repair the caravel as best he could at Grand Canary by making a new rudder for the one lost. He also changed the sails on *La Niña* from lateen to round so she could follow the other two ships with greater ease and less danger.

XII

The Admiral Sails from the Grand Canary on His Voyage of Discovery

WHEN the ships were refitted and ready to sail, on the afternoon of the first of September, he weighed anchor and left Grand Canary. The next day he reached Gomera, where four days more were spent in laying in food, wood, and water. On the next Thursday morning, September 6, 1492, which may be counted as the first day of the ocean voyage, the Admiral left Gomera and sailed away to the west. But he made little way because of the calm. On Sunday about daylight, he found himself nine leagues west of the island Ferro, where they lost sight of land. Many, fearing it would be long before they should see it again, sighed and wept.

The Admiral comforted them all with great promises of lands and riches. To raise their hopes and lessen their fears of a long voyage, he pretended they had sailed fifteen leagues that day although he knew it was eighteen. He decided to keep a short reckoning all the voyage, so the men would not think themselves as far from Spain as they were. Secretly he would keep a record of how far it truly was.

Continuing on his voyage, on the twelfth of September, about sunset, about one hundred and fifty leagues west of Ferro, he discovered a large piece of a mast from a ship of perhaps 120 tons, which seemed to have been in the water a long time. There and somewhat farther the current ran strongly toward the northeast.

When he had gone fifty leagues more to the west, on the thirteenth of September, he found that at nightfall the compass needle was half a point to the northwest of the North Star and at daybreak was a bit more than a point to the northeast. From this he learned that the needle does not point to the North Star, but at some other fixed point. No man had observed this before, so he had reason to be surprised. He was more amazed the third day after, when he was almost one hundred leagues farther west. At night the needles varied a point to the north-

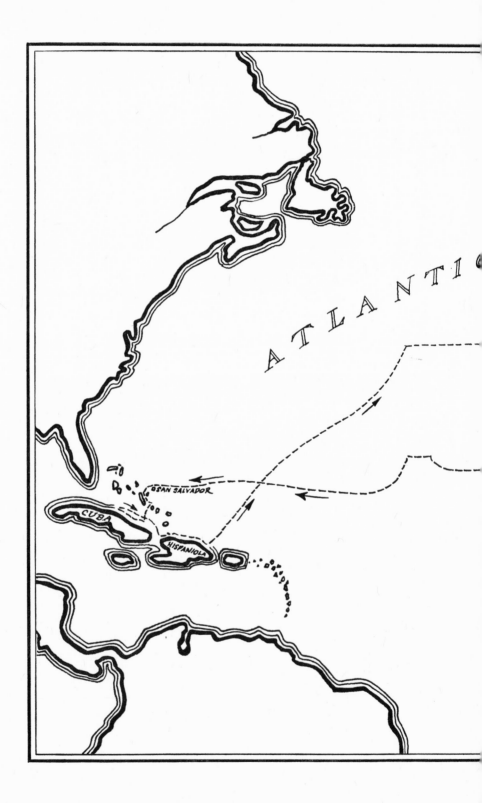

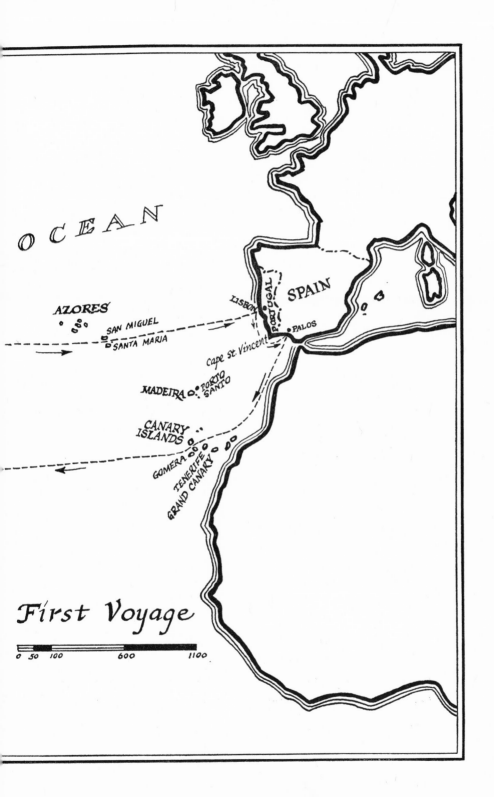

OCEAN

SPAIN

PORTUGAL

LISBON

PALOS

AZORES

SAN MIGUEL

SANTA MARIA

Cape St. Vincent

MADEIRA • PORTO
SANTO

CANARY
ISLANDS

GOMERA
TENERIFE
GRAND CANARY

First Voyage

0 50 100   600   1100

west, while in the morning they pointed to the North Star.

On Saturday night, the fifteenth of September, almost three hundred leagues west of Ferro, they saw a wonderful flash of light fall from the sky into the sea, about four or five leagues from the ships toward the southwest, although the weather was fair, like April, the wind favorable from the northeast and the currents running to the northeast.

The men aboard the caravel *La Niña* told the Admiral that on Friday they had seen a *garjao* [arctic tern or young boatswain bird] and another sort of bird called *rabo de junco* [the boatswain bird] which they were amazed at, as they were the first birds they had seen. They were more surprised the next day, Sunday, at the great abundance of yellowish-green weed covering the surface, which seemed to be newly washed from some island or reef. They saw enough of these weeds the next day to make many swear they were already near land, especially since they saw a live crab among these weeds. That night many tuna fish followed them, running alongside and sticking close to them. The men aboard the caravel *La Niña* killed one with a harpoon.

Now three hundred and fifty leagues west of Ferro, they saw another *rabo de junco,* named this because of the long feathers in its tail like rushes. On the following Tuesday, the eighteenth of September, Martín Alonso Pinzón, who had gone ahead with the *Pinta,* which was a fast sailer, lay to and waited for the Admiral. He said he had seen a great number of birds fly away westward, and because of that he hoped to find land that night. He thought he saw land to the northward at sunset, fifteen leagues distance, covered by dark clouds. All the men wanted the Admiral to go look for the land, but he knew for certain it was not land and would not waste time looking. They had not come to the place where his calculations showed they should find land. The wind now freshened and they had to take in their topsails that night after having run before the wind for eleven days under full sail.

XIII

How All the Men Kept a Sharp Lookout for Signs of Land

A S SUCH a voyage was strange to them and they feared the dangers because they were so far from any help, some began to grumble and mutter. Seeing nothing but sky and water, they looked carefully at everything that came along. They were farther away from land than anyone had ever been before. For this reason I shall tell everything they saw on this first voyage. On any other voyage such little things would not be worth the telling.

On the morning of the nineteenth of September a pelican flew over the Admiral's ship. Others flew over in the afternoon. He began to hope for land, as he thought the birds would not fly very far from it. With these hopes, as soon as the wind died down somewhat, they sounded with two hundred fathoms of line. They found no bottom, but they noticed the current now ran southwest.

On Thurday the twentieth of September, two hours before noon, two pelicans came to the ship, and another one later. Besides, they caught a bird like a heron, only it was black with a white tuft on the head and feet like a duck. They also caught a little fish and saw much seaweed. About daybreak three land birds came to the ship, singing. At sunrise they flew away, which was encouraging. The other fowl were large and used to the water. They might go far from land, but these little ones could not come far.

Three hours later they saw another pelican that came from the west-northwest. In the afternoon of the next day they saw another *rabo de junco* and a pelican. More sea-

weed was seen than before, toward the north as far as they could see. The seaweed was a comfort because they thought it might come from some near land. But it also made them afraid. It was so thick it slowed the ships. As fear makes things worse than they are, they had the notion that what is said to have happened to St. Amador in the frozen sea might happen to them. They might not be able to move backward or forward. So they steered away from the seaweed as much as they could.

But to return to the signs: the next day they saw a whale. On the Saturday following, the twenty-second of September, they saw some gray gulls. The wind blew out of the southwest for three days, sometimes more to the west. Though this was a contrary wind, the Admiral said he looked upon it as a good sign and a help to them.

The men muttered with fear. They said since the wind was always at their backs, they were afraid they never would have a favorable wind to take them home to Spain. Though sometimes the wind did blow from the other direction, they said it was not steady nor strong enough to stir up good-sized waves. It would never carry them back as far as they had to sail. The Admiral used the best argument he could. He told them the land was near and did not allow the waves to build up. But they would not believe him. The Admiral stood in need of God's help just as Moses did when he led the Jews out of Egypt. They did not lay violent hands on Moses because of the deeds God worked through him. So God worked through the Admiral and saved him.

On the Sunday following, the wind started up at westnorthwest with as rough a sea as any of the men could wish. Three hours before noon a turtledove flew over the

ship, and in the afternoon they saw a pelican, a little river
bird, other white birds, and some crabs in the seaweed.
The next day they saw another pelican, several small birds
from the west, and small fish, some of which the sailors
took with harpoons, as they would not bite a hook.

XIV

How the Men Talked Mutiny,
but Other Signs and Tokens
of Land Encouraged Them

THE MORE these signs turned out to be fruitless the
more the crew grew fearful and grumbled. They met
together in the holds of the ships, saying the Admiral in
his mad fantasy planned to make himself a great lord by
risking their lives — or to die in the attempt. They had
tried their luck as much as duty required and gone farther from land and any hope of help than any others had
done. They ought not to destroy themselves, nor go on
with the voyage. If they continued, they would have cause
to be sorry. Food and water would fall short. The ships
had so many leaks and had so much wrong with them
that even now they were hardly fit to go back as far as
they had come. None would blame them for going back.

They would be looked on as very brave men for going on such a voyage and venturing so far. The Admiral being a foreigner without friends at Court, and so many wise and learned men having condemned his ideas, there would be nobody now to favor and defend him. If they accused him of ignorance and poor management, they would be believed sooner than he — no matter what he said.

A few even said they had heard enough talk. In case he would not agree to go back, throw him overboard. They could say later he fell into the sea while taking a sighting on the stars. Nobody would look into the truth of it. It was the best way to return home and to safety.

So they went on from day to day, muttering, complaining, and plotting. The Admiral became worried about their dark mood. At times he spoke fair words to them; at other times, risking death, he threatened to punish any who hindered the voyage. In this way he quieted their fears somewhat and stopped their ill designs. To make them more hopeful, he reminded them of the signs and tokens, and assured them they would soon find land. They watched so carefully they thought every hour a year until they saw land.

On Tuesday the twenty-fifth of September, about sunset, as the Admiral was talking with Pinzón, whose ship was very near, Pinzón cried out all of a sudden, "Land! Land, Sir! The reward is mine!" He pointed toward the southwest and a shape that looked very much like an island, about twenty-five leagues from the ships.

This was so pleasing to the men that they returned thanks to God. The Admiral himself thought it might be land until nightfall. To please the men and keep them

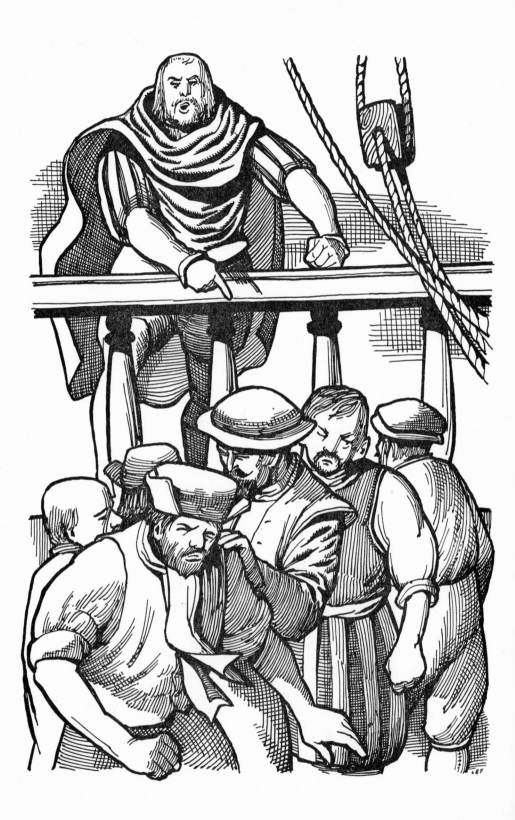

happy, he sailed that way for most of the night. Next morning they realized that what they had seen was only clouds, which often look like land. So, to the disappointment of most of the sailors, they turned the ships westward, as they had always done except when the wind was contrary.

Watchful of signs, they saw a pelican, *rabo de junco* and other birds like those mentioned. On Thursday the twenty-seventh of September, in the morning, they saw another pelican flying west to east and saw many fish with gilded backs, one of which they took with a harpoon. A *rabo de junco* flew by them and they found that the currents for those last days were not so regular as before, but turned with the tide. There was not so much seaweed as before. On Friday all the ships took some fish with gilded backs. On Saturday they saw a frigate bird. Though it is a seabird, it does not rest on the water. It flies through the air pursuing the pelicans, till it makes them drop their excrement from fear, which it catches in the air for food while at sea. It is said to be common near the Cape Verde Islands. Soon after, they saw two pelicans and many flying fish, which are about a span long and have two little wings like a bat. They fly about the height of a lance above the water in a path like a harquebus shot and sometimes they dropped on the ships. After noon they saw much seaweed lying north and south in a line, as they had seen before. Three pelicans and a *rabo de junco* followed them.

On Sunday four *rabos de junco* came to the ship. Because they were together, it was thought land was near, especially since a little while later four pelicans flew by. Also they saw a great many emperor fish which look like the fish called *chopos* that have a hard skin and are not fit to eat.

But no matter how much the Admiral noticed these signs, he never forgot those in the heavens and always studied the stars. He saw with amazement that in this region the Guards of the Little Dipper were directly to the west at nightfall and directly northeast at daybreak. From this he gathered that their whole night's course was only nine astronomical hours, and this was true of every night. He also noticed that at nightfall the compass varied a whole point to the northwest, while at dawn it pointed directly at the polestar. The pilots were disturbed and confused by this, till he told them the cause of it was the circle the polestar made around the north pole. This partly calmed their fears. Such a change from what they knew made them fear danger in such a strange place so far from home.

XV

The Men Try to Make the Admiral Change Course

ON MONDAY the first of October, after sunrise, a pelican came to the ships, and two more about ten in the morning. Long streams of seaweed lay from east to west. In the morning of that day the pilot of the Admiral's ship said they were 578 leagues west of the island Ferro in the Canaries. The Admiral said by his count they were 584, but his secret count was 707, which was 129 leagues more than the pilot reckoned. The other two ships differed very much in their reckoning. The pilot of the caravel *Niña* on the following Wednesday afternoon said they had sailed 540 leagues. The pilot of the caravel *Pinta* said 634. Adding all they had sailed in three days, they were still much short of the truth, for they had always sailed with a good wind at their backs. The Admiral told no one of the pilots' mistaken reckoning, for his men might become more frightened, finding themselves so far from home.

The next day, the second of October, they saw many fish and caught a small tunny. A white bird, like a gull, was seen, and many *pardelas*. They saw some seaweed that was old and almost reduced to powder.

The next day, not seeing any other birds than a few *pardelas,* they were much afraid they had passed between some islands without seeing them. The birds they had seen must have been going from one island to another. The men wanted to steer one way or the other to look for the land they thought must lie there. The Admiral opposed them. He did not want to lose the favorable wind that was carrying him due west on the course he believed to be the best and surest route to the Indies. Besides, running from one place to another looking for what he had always claimed he knew where to find would be less to his credit and standing. The men were ready to mutiny, muttering and plotting against him. But it pleased God to come to his help by fresh tokens. On the afternoon of Thursday, the fourth of October, a flock of more than forty *pardelas* and two pelicans came so close to the ships that a ship's boy hit one with a stone. Before this they had seen a bird like a *rabo de junco,* and another like a seagull, and many flying fish fell into the ships. The next day another *rabo de junco* and a pelican came to the ships. Many *pardelas* were seen.

Sunday the seventh of October, after sunrise, they saw what looked like land to the westward. Since it could not be seen clearly, no man cried it out, not so much from fear of shame at being proved wrong as fear of losing the 10,-000 maravedís a year Their Catholic Majesties had promised for life at the first to sight land. To keep the men from crying "land, land" all the time and causing a short-lived joy, the Admiral ordered that anyone claiming to see land who did not make good his claim in three days, would lose the reward even if he really sighted it later. All aboard being warned, none of them dared to cry out. But the *Niña,* which sailed best, went ahead, fired a gun and put out colors as a sign she had sighted land.

But the farther they sailed the more their spirits sank, until the imagined land faded away. However, it pleased God soon after to give them some manner of comfort. They saw great flights of birds, or more kinds than they had seen before, and flocks of small land birds flying from the west toward the southwest. The Admiral, being now so far from Spain, and sure that such small birds would not go far from land, altered his course and stood to the southwest. He noted this was only a slight change from his first plan and he only copied the Portuguese who made most of their island discoveries by watching the flights of birds. Also, the birds they saw were flying in almost the same direction where he had always expected land to be found. As the men well knew, he had often told them he never expected to find land till they were seven hundred and fifty leagues west of the Canaries.

As they were very near land, they saw many birds of all kinds. On Monday the eighth of October, twelve singing birds of several colors, of the kind that sing in the fields, came to the ship, flew about for a while, and went on their way. The other ships also sighted many birds flying to the southwest. That night many large birds were seen and flights of small birds coming from the north and following the rest. Besides, they saw a good number of tunny fish. In the morning they saw a *garjao,* a pelican, ducks, and small birds flying the same way as the others. They noted the air to be as fresh and full of pleasant odors as Seville in April.

They were now so eager to see land that no sign was enough. Though on Wednesday the tenth of October they saw many birds pass both day and night, the men did not stop complaining nor the Admiral stop blaming them for want of courage. He told them Their Catholic Majesties had sent them to the Indies on this undertaking and they must see it through, for better or worse.

XVI

How the Admiral Sighted the First Land

ON THE afternoon of Thursday, October eleventh, Our Lord, seeing what difficulty the Admiral had in facing his many opponents, was pleased to give clear signs that they were near land. The men took heart. On the *Santa María* they saw a green branch pass near the ship, and then a great green fish of the sort that does not go far from the rocks. Those aboard the *Pinta* saw a cane and a staff, and took from the water another staff skillfully carved, a small board, and much weed of the kind that grows on shore. The *Niña*'s crew saw other such tokens, and a thorny branch loaded with red berries, which seemed to be newly broken off.

These tokens and his own reasoning convinced the Admiral he was near land. That night after they had sung *Salve Regina,* as seamen are accustomed to do at nightfall, he spoke to the men. Our Lord had shown favor to them by bringing them on so long a voyage with fair wind and clear sailing. He asked them to be very watchful that night, reminding them of his first instructions issued to every ship in the Canaries. He had ordered that when they had sailed seven hundred leagues to the westward, without discovering land, they would not sail from midnight to morning. The great desire of all to see land made him risk it now, but they must make up for this daring by keeping a sharp lookout, as his hopes were most high of finding land that night. To him who first sighted land the Admiral would give a velvet doublet in addition to the 10,000 maravedís a year for life Their Highnesses had promised.

After this, at about ten o'clock, as the Admiral stood in the sterncastle, he saw a light ashore, but said it was so unsure a thing that he dared not say it was land. He called Pedro Gutiérrez, butler to the King, and asked if he saw the light. He said he did. They called Rodrigo Sánchez of Segovia to look that way, but he was too slow in coming to the place where the light could be seen to see it. They saw it only once or twice afterward, which

made them think it might be a light or torch belonging to some fisherman or traveller, who lifted it up and let it fall. Perhaps they were people going from one house to another, for the light came and went so quickly that few believed it to be a sign of land.

Being now very watchful, they held their course. About two o'clock in the morning the *Pinta,* a speedy sailer and far ahead, fired the signal for land. A sailor named Rodrigo de Triana first sighted it while they were two leagues away. The reward money did not go to him, however. It went to the Admiral who had seen the light in the midst of darkness, standing for the spiritual light he was then spreading in those dark regions. Being now near land, they waited, thinking it a long time till morning when they might set eyes on what they had so long desired.

XVII

How the Admiral Went Ashore and Took Possession for Their Catholic Majesties

WHEN DAY came, they saw an island, fifteen leagues in length, level, without hills, full of green trees and many springs, with a large lake in the middle. A multitude of people ran down to the shore, amazed and

marveling at the sight of the ships, which they took for large sea beasts. They were eager to know for sure what the ships were, and the men on board were just as eager to know them. Their wishes were soon satisfied, for the ships came to anchor. The Admiral went ashore with an armed boat, flying the royal standard. The captains of the other two ships came in their boats with the special banners of this expedition, which bore a green cross with an F on one side for Ferdinand and a Y on the other for Ysabel, both letters capped with crowns.

Having all given thanks to God, they knelt on the shore and kissed the ground with tears of joy for His great mercy. The Admiral stood up, and called the island San Salvador. After that, he claimed the discovery in the name of Their Catholic Majesties with the proper words and ceremony. The men hailed him as admiral and viceroy. They swore to obey him as the representative of Their Highnesses and showed the happiness and pleasure such a triumph deserved. They asked his pardon for the injuries they had done him out of fear and little faith. Many of the Indians came to watch this celebration and rejoicing, and the Admiral, seeing they were gentle, peaceable, and very simple people, gave them some red caps, strings of glass beads, which they hung about their necks, and other things of small value, which they treasured as if they had been precious stones of great price.

XVIII

What the People the Admiral Called Indians Were Like

THE ADMIRAL returned to his boats with the Indians following, even following him out to the ships by swimming. Others came in canoes, carrying parrots, skeins of spun cotton, darts, and other trifles to barter for glass beads, bells, and other things of small value.

Being a people of primitive simplicity, they went about as naked as they were born. A woman among them wore no more than the rest. Most of them were young, not more than thirty, and of goodly height. Their hair was straight, thick, very black and short, being cut above the ears, except some few who let it grow down to their shoulders and tied it with a strong thread about their heads like a woman's braids. Their faces were pleasant and their features good, but their foreheads were too wide and made them look somewhat wild. They were of medium build, well-shaped, solid, and of an olive color like Canary Islanders, or sunburnt peasants. Some were painted black, some white, and some red. Some painted the face only, others the whole body, and others nothing but the eyes and nose.

They had no weapons like our men, nor did they have

knowledge of them, for when the Christians showed them a naked sword, they took it by the sharp edge and cut themselves. They had no iron, and made the darts mentioned before out of a stick with the point hardened in the fire or armed with a fish's tooth. Some of the Indians had scars about their bodies. Being asked by signs how they got them, they answered by signs that people came on raids from other islands to capture them. They received those wounds in defending themselves. They seemed clever and quick-tongued, for they easily repeated words heard just once. The only animals of any sort were parrots which they carried to barter.

Next day, the thirteenth of October, in the morning many of them came down to the shore and got in their boats, called canoes. These canoes are made of the trunk of a tree hollowed out like a trough. The largest of them hold forty or forty-five men, and they have all sizes down to some that hold only one man. They row with a paddle like a baker's peel for removing bread from the oven. Their oars are not fixed on the side as ours, are, but they dip them in the water and pull back as if they were digging. The canoes are so light and cleverly built that if they are upset, the Indians soon turn them right again while swimming around them. They slosh the water from side to side, and when it is more than half empty, they dip out the rest with gourds cut in half for that purpose.

That day they brought the same kind of things to trade as the day before, giving all they had for any small things they could get. No jewels or any sort of metal was seen among them except some small gold disks which hung from a hole made through the nostrils. Being asked where they got the gold, they answered by signs, from the south where a king had many tiles and vessels of gold. They said to the south and southwest there were many other islands and large countries.

They wanted anything of ours. Being poor and having nothing to give in exchange, as soon as they came aboard, if they could lay a hand on anything, though it be but a piece of broken crockery or glazed bowl, they leaped into the sea and swam ashore. If they brought anything aboard, they would give it all for any little trifle of ours or a bit of broken glass. Some of them gave sixteen skeins of cotton for three small Portuguese copper coins. These skeins weighed more than twenty-five pounds each and the cotton was well spun. Thus they spent the day and at night they all went ashore.

It may be said that their liberality in trading did not come from the great value they put on those things themselves, but they valued them because they were ours, looking on it as most certain that our men had come from heaven, and they wanted to have some token as a memorial of our coming.

XIX

How the Admiral Left That Island and Went to Discover Others

NEXT SUNDAY, the fifteenth of October, the Admiral went along the coast of the island to the northwest in his boats to see what was on the other side. He found a bay or harbor large enough to hold all the ships in Christendom. The Indians, seeing him go by, ran along the shore crying out and promising him provisions. They called others to come and see the people dropped to earth from heaven, and lifted their hands up to heaven as if giving thanks for their coming. Many of them came to the boats, swimming and in canoes. They asked by signs whether they came down from heaven and prayed them to land and rest themselves.

The Admiral gave them all glass beads, pins, and other trifles, rejoicing at their great simplicity. Then he came to a peninsula which would take three days of hard rowing to round. It was habitable and a good fort might be made there. He saw six Indian houses with gardens around them as pleasant as they are in Castile in May. But his men were weary of rowing, and he saw plainly that it was not the land he looked for, nor did it show promise of riches to cause him to stay longer. Taking seven of the Indians to serve him as interpreters, he returned to his ships. He sailed for other islands that he could see from the peninsula, which appeared to be level, green, and well-peopled, as the Indians themselves said.

The next day, Monday the sixteenth of October, he reached Santa María de la Concepción, which was seven leagues distance. That side of the island next to San Salvador runs five leagues from north to south, but the Admiral went to that side which runs from east to west and is more than ten leagues long. He anchored toward the western end of the island and landed to do as he had done on San Salvador. The people of the island ran to see the Christians, looking on them in wonder as the others had.

The Admiral saw this island was the same, so the next day he sailed westward to another, much larger island. He anchored on the coast, which runs northwest to southeast for more than twenty-eight leagues. This was like the others, level, with a fine beach. He named it Fernandina.

Before they reached this island and Concepción, they found a man in a small canoe. He had a piece of their kind of bread, a gourd of water, and a little earth that looks like vermillion, which they paint their bodies with. He also had some dry leaves [tobacco] which the Indians value because they have a sweet scent and are supposed to be healthful. In a little basket he had a string of green glass beads and two small Portuguese coins. From this they guessed he had come from San Salvador, had passed Concepción, and was going to Fernandina to carry news of the Christians. But because the way was far and tiring, he came to the ships, was taken up with his canoe and treated kindly by the Admiral. The Admiral planned, as soon as he reached land, to send him ashore, which he did, so he might spread the news.

The good report of the Christians the Indian gave caused the people of Fernandina to come aboard in their canoes. They traded the same sort of thing they did before, for these people were like the rest. When the boat went ashore for water, the Indians very readily showed where it was and carried small caskfuls to the large barrels in the boat. They seemed to be wiser and shrewder than the first, thus they bargained harder for what they traded. They had cotton cloth in their houses which they put on their beds. Some of the women covered their private parts with short hanging cloths and others with woven cloth wrapped around them.

Among other notable things they saw on the island were

some trees that had leaves and branches of four or five different kinds that seemed not to be grafted on, but growing naturally. They also saw fishes of several shapes and fine colors, but no land animals other than lizards and a few snakes. To explore the island better, they sailed to the northwest and came to the mouth of a beautiful harbor. There was a small island at the entrance with shallow water on both sides, so they could not get in. They did not much care, for they wanted to be near a village close by.

Although this was the largest island they had yet seen, they found only twelve or fifteen houses together, built like tents. They saw no furniture or any ornaments other than what they carried to the ships to trade. For beds they used a kind of net in the shape of a sling, tied to two houseposts. Here they saw some dogs like mastiffs and others like beagles, but none of them could bark.

XX

How the Admiral Sailed to Other Islands That Were in Sight

FINDING nothing of value on Fernandina, they sailed on Friday the nineteenth of October to another called Saometo, which he named Isabella. Here are the names he gave the islands, in order. The first, which the Indians

called Guanahaní, he named San Salvador in honor of
God, who had shown it to him and saved him from many
dangers. The second, for his own devotion to the Virgin
Mary and because she is the great patroness of all Christians, he called Santa María de la Concepción. The third
he called Fernandina in honor of the Catholic King, the
fourth Isabella in honor of the Catholic Queen, and
the island that he found next, Cuba, he called Juana for
Prince Juan, heir to the throne of Castile. Thus he aimed
to honor both spiritual and worldly powers in these
names.

It is true, he says, that as to goodness, size, and beauty,
Fernandina surpassed the rest. Besides abounding in
springs of delicious water, pleasant meadows and trees,
there were some hills, which the others lacked, being

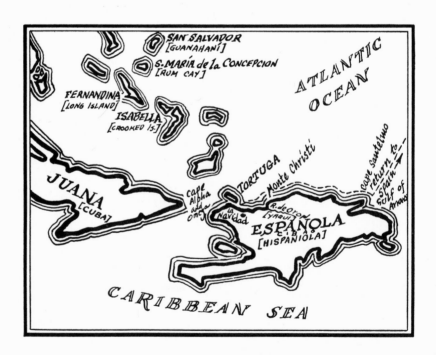

level. The Admiral was charmed by its beauty, and to perform the ceremony of taking possession, he landed on some meadows as delightful as they are in Spain in April. They heard the song of the nightingale and other small birds, a song so sweet the Admiral could not bear to leave. Not only were the birds in the trees, but flew through the air in such swarms that they darkened the sun. Most of them differed from our birds.

There are many streams and lakes, and near one of them they saw a serpent seven feet long and more than a foot wide in the belly. Being disturbed by our men, it threw itself into the lake. The lake was not deep, so they killed it with their pikes, not without dread and wonder, for it had a fierce and frightful look. Afterward they came to look on it as a delicacy, the best food the Indians had. When the horrid skin and scales that cover it are taken off, the flesh is very white, soft and tasty. The Indians call them iguanas.

Wanting to know more about that country and it being late, they left the iguana there until the next day. Journeying through that country, they found a town, where the people had fled, carrying away as much of their goods as they could. The Admiral would not allow his men to take anything of what they had left, so the Indians would not look upon the Christians as thieves. Also they might get over their fear and come willingly to the ships to trade, as the others had done.

XXI

The Admiral Discovers Cuba and Tries to Learn of Its People

HAVING learned the secrets of the island Isabella and the ways of the people, the Admiral did not want to lose any more time among those islands. As the Indians said, they were all very much alike. Therefore he set sail with a fair wind for a very large country much praised by them, called Cuba, which lay to the south. On Sunday the twenty-eighth of October, he reached the coast on the north side. This island from the first sight looked better and richer than the others because of its hills and mountains, variety of trees, large plains, and the extent of its coasts and beaches.

To get some knowledge of its people, the Admiral anchored in a large river, where the trees were very thick and tall, bearing fruits and flowers differing from ours, and filled with birds. The place was delightful for the grasses were tall and not like those of Spain. Though our men knew such kinds as wheat, purslane, and the like, yet they did not know the varieties of this island. Going to two houses that were not far off, they found the people had fled in fear, leaving their nets and all other fishing tackle, and one of their barkless dogs. As the Admiral ordered, nothing was touched. It was enough for him now just to see what their food and necessities of life were.

Returning to their ships, they held on their course westward and came to another river which the Admiral called Río de Mares or River of Seas. This was much larger than the other, because a ship could go up it. The shores were thickly inhabited, but the people, seeing the ships, fled toward the mountains, which were high, round and covered with trees. The Indians took all they could carry with them.

The Admiral was unable to learn anything about the island because of the people's fear. If he landed with many men, it would make them more afraid. He decided to send two men with one of the Indians brought from San Salvador and the Indian taken on board with his canoe. He ordered them to travel inland, be friendly with the Indians, and find out all they could. So no time would be lost while waiting, he ordered his ships laid on their sides on the shore to be caulked.

XXII

How the Two Christians Returned
and What They Reported

O N NOVEMBER the fifth, the ships having been
     repaired and ready to sail, the two Christians re-
turned with the two Indians. They said they had traveled
twelve leagues inland and came to a town of fifty pretty
large houses made of wood and covered with palm leaves.
They looked like tents, as the others had. About a thousand people lived there, for all of one family lived under
one roof.

The principal men came out to meet them and led them
by the arms to the town. They gave them the best house to
stay in, where they had them sit down on seats made of
one piece in strange shapes, almost like some creature with
short legs and the tail lifted up to lean against, as broad
as the seat. The chair had a head in front with golden eyes
and ears. The Christians being seated, all the Indians sat
about them on the ground and came up one by one to kiss
their hands and feet, believing they came from heaven.
The Indians gave them some boiled roots to eat not unlike chestnuts in taste [sweet potatoes or yams]. They
begged them to stay there among them, or at least rest five

or six days, because the two Indians whom they brought along as interpreters spoke well of them. Soon after, many women came in to see them and the men went out. With equal respect they kissed their feet and hands, offering them the gifts they had brought.

When the time came to return to the ships, many Indians wanted to go with them, but they would only allow the King, his son, and one servant. The Admiral treated them honorably. The Christians told the Admiral that going and coming back they had found several towns where they were welcomed in the same friendly manner, but none of them had more than five houses. Along the way they met many people who always carried a firebrand to light certain herbs [tobacco] they carried along with them, the smoke of which they inhale, and to roast the roots which are their principal food.

They also saw many kinds of trees and plants which were not seen on the seacoast. They saw a great variety of birds, differing from ours, but among them were partridges and nightingales. As for four-footed animals, they had seen none but barkless dogs. There was a great deal of tilled land, some planted with those roots, a kind of bean, and a sort of grain they call maize [corn], which tasted good when baked, boiled, or ground into meal. They saw vast quantities of cotton, well-spun and in skeins. In one house they saw more than 12,500 pounds of woven cotton. The plant it comes from is not planted, but grows wild about the fields like roses and opens when ripe. But not all open at the same time, for on one plant they saw a little bud, another just open, and a third fully ripe and ready to fall. The Indians afterward carried great quantities aboard the ships, and gave a basketful for a leather thong. None of them use it to clothe themselves, but only to make nets for beds, which they call *hamacas* [hammocks], and in weaving the cloths with which the women cover their private parts. Being asked whether they had gold or pearls or spice, they made signs that there was great plenty to the east, in a country called Bohío [Hispaniola], but we did not know yet for certain what place they meant.

XXIII

The Admiral Stops Following the Western Coast of Cuba and Turns East Toward Hispaniola

HEARING this, the Admiral decided to stay no longer in the Rió de Mares. He ordered some natives of Cuba made captive, meaning to take some from each island to Spain to tell of their country. They took twelve men, women, and children, and it was done so peacefully that when they were ready to sail, the husband of one of the women and father of two of the children that had been carried aboard, came to the ships in a canoe. He asked by signs to be taken along with them and not parted from his wife and children. This pleased the Admiral very much, who ordered that he be taken aboard, and all of them treated well.

That same day, the thirteenth of November, he set sail to the eastward for the island the Indians called Bohío. The wind blowing hard from the north, he was forced to come to anchor again off Cuba, among some high islands lying near a large harbor which he called Puerto del Princípe or the Prince's Port, and where the islands were, El Mar de Nuestra Señora, or the Sea of Our Lady.

These islands lay so thick and close there was not more than a quarter of a league from one to another, and about a musket shot for the most part. The channels were so deep and the shores so adorned with trees and greenery that it was delightful sailing down them. Among a multitude of other trees were palms with smooth green trunks.

Although these islands were not inhabited, there were signs of many fires made by fishermen. As we learned afterward, the people of Cuba go in great numbers by canoe over to these islands and other uninhabited islands, living on the fish they catch, the birds, crabs, and other things they find on the earth, for the Indians eat such loathsome things as large fat spiders, white worms that breed in rotten wood and other decaying things. Often they eat their fish almost raw, digging out the eyes to eat before roasting the rest. They eat many other things that would make us sick or kill us if we ate them. They follow the fishing and hunting by the seasons, sometimes on one island and sometimes on another, changing their diet with the island when they get tired of it.

On one of the islands of the Sea of Our Lady, the Christians killed with their swords an animal like a badger [a coati], and in the sea found much mother-of-pearl. Casting their nets, they caught many fish. Among them there was one like a hog, all covered with hard skin, no part of him soft except the tail [a trunkfish]. They also saw that in this sea and the islands the tide rose and fell much more than in other places they had been. Also the tides were the opposite of ours in Spain, for it was low water when the moon was in the southwest by south.

XXIV

The Admiral Sets Sail Again for Hispaniola and One of the Ships Leaves Him to Search for Gold

O N MONDAY the nineteenth of November the Admiral left Puerto del Príncipe and La Mar de Nuestra Señora, steering eastward for the island of Bohío or Hispaniola. But the wind blew against him and he was forced to tack back and forth between the island Isabella and Puerto del Príncipe, which lie almost north and south, twenty-five leagues apart.

During this time, on Wednesday, November twenty-first, Martín Alonso Pinzón, being told by certain Indians he had concealed on his caravel that there was great plenty of gold on the island Bohío, left the Admiral. His desire for gold blinded him, for neither the weather nor anything else kept him from rejoining the Admiral. He could have sailed right up with the wind at his back, but he did not want to. His vessel was an excellent sailer and he made as much way as he could. They had sailed in sight of each other, but on Thursday he went ahead all day and vanished at night.

This left the Admiral with only two ships. The weather

not being fit to sail toward Hispaniola, he returned to Cuba, to another harbor near Puerto del Príncipe, which he called Santa Caterina, to take on wood and water. Here, inland, they found plenty of tall pine trees that would make masts for ships or supply planks to build as many ships as anyone would want. Evergreen oaks and others like those of Castile also grew there.

As the Indians kept directing him to Hispaniola, the Admiral ran along the coast ten or twelve leagues farther toward the southeast, finding excellent harbors and many large rivers along the way. The Admiral says so much of the delightfulness and beauty of that country that I have thought fit to put down his own words in speaking of the mouth of a river which makes a harbor he called Puerto Santo. He says:

When I went with the boats to the mouth of the harbor toward the south, I found a river big enough for a galley to row up. The entrance was so well-hidden it could only be seen when close by. Its beauty invited me to go up it, if only for a boat's length. I found from five to eight fathoms of water. The beauty and delightfulness of the river and the clearness of the water, through which I could see the sand at the bottom, the abundance of palm trees of several sorts, the finest and highest I had yet seen, the boundless number of other large green trees, the birds, the verdure of the fields, drew me farther up the stream and tempted me to stay there forever.

This country, most serene Princes, is so wonderfully fine that it exceeds all other beauty and delightfulness as much as day does night. That is why I often told my companions that no matter how hard I should try to give Your

Highnesses a perfect account of it, my tongue and pen
would always fall short of the truth. I was so struck by the
beauty of it that I could not express it. In writing of other
places, of their trees and fruits, plants and harbors and all
that was in them, I did as well as I could and all the men
swore no country could be more beautiful. But now I must
be silent, wishing others might see this place and try to
write of it. They will see how far they fall short of doing
it justice.

The Admiral went on with his boats and saw a canoe
among the trees of the harbor, drawn up under a boat-
house made of thatch. The canoe was made of the trunk
of a single tree and was as big as a twelve-oar boat. In
some nearby houses they found a cake of wax and a man's
skull hung in two baskets on a post. Later they found the
same thing in another house, which made them think the
skull must be that of an ancestor of the family living in
the house. But they could find no Indians to learn anything, for as soon as they saw the Christians, they fled
from their houses to the other side of the harbor. After-
wards our men found another canoe about seventy feet
long that would carry fifty men, made like the other
spoken of before.

XXV

They Reach Hispaniola and Find Many Indians

THE ADMIRAL sailed one hundred and six leagues eastward along the coast of Cuba until he came to the easternmost point, which he called Alpha and Omega, the beginning or the end, depending on whether you were sailing east or west. On Wednesday the fifth of December, he set out for Hispaniola, sixteen leagues to the east of Cuba. Because of some currents, he could not reach it till next day, when he put in to what he called Port St. Nicholas, because it was that saint's feast day. The port is large, deep, safe, and surrounded by trees. The country is rockier and the trees smaller than those they had seen so far, like those of Castile. Among them were small oaks, myrtle, and other shrubs. A pleasant river ran along a plain into the harbor, which had canoes as large as fifteen-oar boats all about it.

The Admiral, not being able to meet any of the people, went along the coast northward, until he came to a harbor that he called Puerto de la Concepción, which lies almost due south of a small island about the size of Grand Canary, which he named Tortuga [turtle]. Seeing that this island of Bohío was very large, that the land and trees were like those of Spain [España], and that the sailors caught several fishes like those of Spain, such as sole, skate, salmon, shad, sardines, and crabs, he give it the name of Española [in English Hispaniola].

As they were very curious about the nature of the island, while some were fishing on the shore, three Christians went into the woods and ran into a group of naked Indians. Seeing the Christians come near, the Indians, in a great fright, ran into the thickest of the woods, which they did easily, not having any clothing to slow them down. The Christians ran after them, as they needed an interpreter, but they could only overtake a young woman who wore nothing but a gold nose plug. She was carried to the ship, where the Admiral gave her several trinkets

and sent her ashore unharmed. He ordered three Indians of those he brought with him and three Christians to go with her to the town where she lived.

The next day he sent eleven well-armed men ashore, who, after travelling four leagues, found a sort of town or village of more than a thousand houses scattered about a valley. The inhabitants seeing them coming, fled into the woods. The Indian guide that our men had brought from San Salvador went after them, calling for them to return, and speaking so well of the Christians, swearing they came from heaven, that he persuaded them to turn back quietly without fear. Afterward, full of wonder, they would lay their hands on our men's heads to honor them, bring them food, and give them anything they might want, without asking anything in return. They begged them to stay the night in their village. The Christians would not accept the invitation, but returned to their ships, carrying the news that the country was very pleasant and abounding in the food of the Indians. The people were lighter-skinned and better looking than any they had yet seen in the islands. They were friendly and courteous. They said the land where gold could be found lay farther eastward.

The Admiral hearing this report, set sail immediately though the wind was against him. On the Sunday following, the fifteenth of December, as he was tacking back and forth between Hispaniola and Tortuga, he found an Indian alone in a little canoe. They were all amazed that he was not swallowed up by the sea, the wind and waves were so high. The Admiral took him into his ship, carried him to Hispaniola and set him ashore with several gifts. He told the Indians how kindly he had been treated and spoke so well of the Christians that many of them came aboard right away. But they brought nothing of value, except some small pieces of gold hanging at their ears and noses. Being asked where they got the gold, they told by signs that there was much of it farther south.

The next day a great canoe with forty men in it came from the island Tortuga, which was near the place where the Admiral lay at anchor. The cacique or lord of that harbor of Hispaniola was on the shore trading a large piece of gold he had brought. When the cacique saw the canoe, they all sat on the ground as a sign of peace. Most of the men in the canoe leaped ashore as if they wanted to fight. The cacique arose with threatening words and made them return to the canoe. He splashed water at them and picked up pebbles on the beach, which he threw at the men in the canoe. The cacique took a pebble and handed it to a servant of the Admiral to throw at the canoe to show the Admiral took the cacique's side. The servant could not throw it as the canoe went away quickly. After this, talking about the island the Admiral called Tortuga, the cacique swore that there was more gold than on Hispaniola, and about fifteen days' journey from where they were there was more gold than in any other place.

XXVI

How the Cacique Came Aboard in a Stately Manner

ON TUESDAY the eighteenth of December, a cacique who lived five leagues from where the ships lay, came in the morning to the town near the sea. Some of the Spaniards were there by the Admiral's order to see whether the Indians brought more gold. Seeing the cacique come, they went to tell the Admiral, saying he did not come on foot but on a litter carried by four young men who showed him great respect though he was very young. He brought two hundred attendants with him.

After reaching the beach, he rested a while, then came aboard the Admiral's ship with his people. The Admiral himself writes this about the visit:

Your Highnesses would no doubt have been pleased to see his dignity and what respect his people paid him, though all of them were naked. When he came aboard and learned I was having dinner at the table below the sterncastle, he came right in and sat beside me without giving me time to go out to welcome him or to rise from table. When he came down, he made signs to all his followers to

stay above, which they did with the greatest readiness and respect in the world, sitting down on the deck, except two old men who seemed to be his counselors, who sat at his feet. I thought he might like to try our food, so I ordered some brought to him. He tasted of everything and sent the rest to his men, and they all ate some of it. He did the same with the drink, only pressing it to his lips and passing it to the others, all with great dignity and few words. What he said, from all that I could gather, was very weighty and sensible. The two old men watched him closely, speaking to and for him with great respect.

After eating, one of his gentlemen brought him a belt not unlike those used in Castile, though differently made, which he took in his hands and gave me with two pieces of wrought gold, which was very thin, so I believe there is very little gold here, though the place where it comes from is near and has much. I saw that he eyed a counterpane that lay on my bed, so I gave it to him with some fine amber beads I had about my neck, with a pair of red shoes and a bottle of orange-water. He was wonderfully pleased, and both he and his counselors were much troubled because they did not understand me nor I them. I did make out, however, that if I wanted anything, all the island was at my command.

I sent for a letter-case in which I carried a gold coin with Your Highnesses likeness on it and showed it to him, saying again that Your Highnesses were mighty Princes and ruled over the best part of the world. I showed him the royal banners and the others with the cross. He was greatly impressed, and turning to his counselors, said Your Highnesses were certainly mighty Princes, since you had sent me such a great distance from Heaven. Much passed between us which I did not understand, but I could tell that everything he saw filled him with wonder.

As it was now late and he wished to go, I sent him ashore in my boat with great honor and had several guns fired. When he reached shore, he got into his litter attended by two hundred men and his son was carried on the shoulders of an important man. He ordered that all the Spaniards ashore be given food and receive very courteous treatment. Afterward a sailor who met him on the path told me that all the things I had given him were carried before him by a man of great worth, and that his son did not go along the road with him, but followed at some distance with as many attendants as he had. A brother of his came on foot with nearly as many more, with two important men supporting him under the arms. I had given him some small things when he came aboard after his brother.

XXVII

The Loss of the Santa María

THE ADMIRAL continues, saying that on Monday the twenty-fourth of December, the weather was very calm with hardly any wind, just enough to carry him from the Sea of Santo Tomás to about a league beyond Punta Santa, the Holy Cape. About eleven o'clock at night, at the end of the first watch, he went to his cabin to rest, for he had not slept in two days and a night. The weather being calm, the seaman turned the tiller over to a grummet, or ship's boy, "which," says the Admiral, "I had forbidden during the whole voyage, ordering, whether the wind blew or not, never to leave the helm to a grummet."

To tell the truth, I thought myself safe from shallow water or reefs, for that Sunday when I sent my boats to the king, they went at least three leagues and a half beyond the Punta Santa. The seamen had seen all the coast, with the shoals that lie three leagues east-southeast of that Cape, and charted the course to sail, something that had not been done before during the whole voyage.

It pleased Our Lord that while I lay in bed, the ship in a dead calm, the sea as still as water in a cup, all the men went to rest and left the helm to a grummet. Thus it came to pass that the swells very slowly carried the ship onto one of those reefs on which the waves broke with such a roaring noise it could be heard a league away.

The boy, feeling the rudder strike and hearing the noise, cried out. Hearing him, I got up immediately. I recognized before anyone that we were aground. Right away the ship's master, whose watch it was, came out. I ordered him and other sailors to take the boat the ship was towing and carry our anchor astern. He and many others leaped into a boat, I believing they were doing what I had ordered. But they rowed away to the *Niña* which was half a league off. Seeing that they fled with the boat, that the tide was ebbing, and the ship in danger, I quickly had the masts cut down and lightened ship as much as I could to see if I could get her off the reef. But the tide ebbed still more and the ship could not budge. She began to list, her new seams opened, and she filled with water.

Meanwhile the *Niña*'s boat had come over to help me. The caravel's people, seeing that the men in the *Santa María*'s boat were escaping to save their own necks, would not let them aboard, and they had to return to the ship.

Seeing no way of saving the ship, I went to the *Niña* to save the men. The wind blew from the land, a great part of the night was past, and we did not know our way out of these shoals, so I lay by with the caravel till day came. Then I headed for the ship through the reef, having first sent Diego de Arana of Córdoba, chief constable of the fleet, and Pedro Gutiérrez, to let the king know what had happened: that on my way to visit him as he had asked the last Saturday, I had lost my ship on a reef a league and a half from his town.

Told of our misfortune, the king shed tears and immediately sent all the people in the place in their canoes to the ship. He, together with his brothers and relations kept a careful watch both aboard and ashore to see that everything was done right. From time to time he sent some of his kindred weeping to beg me not to be downcast, for he would give me all he had. I do assure Your Highnesses that better care could not have been taken of our goods in Castile, for we did not lose the value of a pin. He had all our goods placed near his palace, where he kept them till two houses were emptied, which he gave us for storehouses. He placed armed men to guard them, who stood there day and night. All the other natives wept as if our loss were their own.

They are such loving, tractable, generous people that I swear to Your Highnesses there are no better people nor country on earth. They love their neighbors as themselves, and their speech is the sweetest and gentlest in the world, and they always speak with a smile. True, both men and women go as naked as they were born, yet, Your Highnesses may believe me, they have very good customs and the king is served with great state and shows such dignity that it is a pleasure to watch him. And what good memories these people have, and how eager they are to know everything. This moves them to ask many questions about what such a thing is and what is its use.

XXVIII

The Admiral Decides to Plant a Colony Where the King Lived

O N WEDNESDAY the twenty-sixth of December, the chief king of that country came aboard the Admiral's caravel. He expressed much grief and offered anything that might be needed, saying he had already given the Christians three houses to store all that had been taken out of the ship, but would give more if they could use them.

In the meantime, a canoe came with some Indians from another island, bringing pieces of thin sheet-gold to trade for hawks' bells, which they valued more than anything. Also, the seamen returned from shore, saying many Indians had gathered in the town from other places, bringing several gold objects which they traded for lace points and other trifles. They said they would bring more gold if the Christians wanted it. The cacique, seeing this pleased the Admiral, told him he would have a great quantity brought from Cibao, where most of the gold was found.

Before going ashore, he invited the Admiral to dine with him on yams and cassava bread, their principal food.

He gave the Admiral some masks with eyes of gold and large golden ears, and other pretty things that they hang about their necks. He complained of the Caribs who carried away his men to make slaves of them and to eat them. He was much comforted when the Admiral showed him our weapons, saying he would defend the cacique with them. He was most astonished at our cannon, which terrified the Indians so that they fell down as if they were dead when they heard it fired.

The Admiral, finding so much kindness among these people and such signs of gold, almost forgot his grief over the loss of his ship. He thought God must have brought it to pass so that he might establish a colony there. He could leave some of his men to get more knowledge of the country and the people by trading with the village and learning their language. When he returned from Spain with more men and supplies, he would have somebody to guide him in settling and conquering that country. He was even more inclined to do this because many volunteered gladly to stay and settle. He decided to build a town with the timbers of the *Santa María,* of which nothing else was left, everything of any use having been taken out of it.

Next day, the twenty-seventh of December, news was brought that the *Pinta* was in a river toward the eastern point of the island. To make sure, the cacique, whose name was Guacanagarí, sent a canoe with some Indians and a Christian. They went twenty leagues along the coast, but returned without any news of it. They did not believe the Indian who said he had seen it several days before. Nevertheless, the Admiral did not change his mind about leaving some Christians at La Navidad, for the Indians kept bringing masks of gold to give them and telling them of several provinces on the island where gold was found.

As the Admiral was now ready to leave, he talked with the king about the Caribs and his fear of them. To make him pleased with having the Christians there and to make him afraid of our arms, he had a lombard shot fired through the hull of the *Santa María*. This terrified the cacique. Besides, he showed him all our other weapons, explaining how some were used for offense and some for defense. He told him he was leaving these arms for his defense, and he need not fear the Caribs, for the Christians would kill them all. He himself would return to Castile for jewels and other things to give him. Then he particularly recommended Diego de Arana, son of Rodrigo de Arana, mentioned above. To Diego, to Pedro Gutiérrez, and to Rodrigo de Escobedo, he left the government of the fort and command of thirty-six men, a great store of trade goods and supplies, arms and cannon, and the *Santa María*'s boat. He left carpenters, caulkers, and other men necessary for settling there, such as a surgeon, a tailor, and a gunner. This done, he prepared with all possible speed to return directly to Castile without making any more discoveries. He feared, since he had but one ship left, some other misfortune might befall him, which would keep Their Catholic Majesties from coming to know of those kingdoms he had newly gained for them.

XXIX

The Admiral Sets Out for Spain and Finds the Pinta

ON FRIDAY the fourth of January at sunrise, the Admiral set sail from the port he had named La Navidad [the Nativity] because he had landed there on Christmas Day, escaping the dangers of the sea, and began building his little colony. He set a course to the northwest with the *Niña*'s boat going ahead to guide him through the reefs and shoals. These shallows reach from Cape Santo to Cape Serpent, which is six leagues, and runs out to sea more than three leagues. The coast is all beach and plain for four leagues inland, then rises to high mountains. There are many villages larger than those on other islands.

Then he sailed toward a high mountain which he called Monte Cristi, that lies eighteen leagues east of Cape Santo. So whoever would go to La Navidad, when he discovers Monte Cristi, which is round like a tent and looks like a rock, must keep out at sea two leagues from it and sail west till he comes to Cape Santo. Then he will be five leagues from La Navidad, and should follow some channels through the shoals. The Admiral thought it fit to mention these facts so the location of the first Christian town in the Western World might be known.

They sailed east of Monte Cristi against the wind. On Sunday the sixth of January, in the morning, a sailor sent aloft saw the *Pinta,* sailing westward with the wind. Coming up with the Admiral, the captain, Martín Alonso Pinzón, came aboard the *Niña* and began inventing reasons and making up excuses for leaving him, saying it had happened against his will. The Admiral, although he knew it was not true and was aware of his hostility toward him, remembering his insolence earlier in the voyage, thought it best to pretend to believe him, for fear the whole undertaking would come to ruin. Which might very well have happened, because most of the crew were Martín Alonso's townsmen and many were his kinsmen.

The truth is, that when Martín Alonso left the Admiral at the island of Cuba, he went away with the design to sail to the island of Babeque, because the Indians aboard his caravel told him much gold was there. When he got there and found nothing, he returned to Hispaniola, where other Indians told him the gold was. He spent twenty days in sailing no more than fifteen leagues east of La Navidad, to a river the Admiral called River of Grace. Martín Alonso stayed there sixteen days and found plenty of gold, trading trifles for it. He gave half the gold to his crew to please them and to get their agreement to his keeping the rest as captain. Later he tried to make the Admiral think he knew nothing of the gold.

The Admiral, following his course, came to anchor at Monte Cristi. As the wind was against him and he could not sail, he went exploring up a river southwest of the mountain in his boat. Because he found much gold dust in the sands of the river, he called it Río de Oro. This river lies seventeen leagues east of La Navidad and is not much smaller than the Guadalquivir that runs through Córdoba.

XXX

A Skirmish with the Indians

ON SUNDAY the thirteenth of January, being off Cape Enamorado, the Admiral sent a party ashore in the boat, where they found some fierce-looking Indians with bows and arrows. They seemed to be ready to fight, but at the same time seemed surprised. However, after some parley, our men managed to buy two of their bows and a few arrows. With much difficulty they got one of them to go aboard the *Niña* to speak with the Admiral. Their speech matched their fierce appearance, which was fiercer than that of any people they had met. Their faces were smudged with charcoal as it is the custom of all those people to paint themselves, some black, some red, and some white, some one way and some another. Their hair was very long and hung in nets made of parrots' feathers.

One of them, standing before the Admiral as naked as he was born, said in a haughty voice that all the people in those parts went about as he did. The Admiral, thinking this was one of the Caribs and that the bay parted them from Hispaniola, asked him where the Caribs lived. He pointed his finger and said on islands to the east and that there were pieces of guanin [an alloy of gold and copper] as big as half the stern of the *Niña*. He told them that the island of Matinino was inhabited by women only, with whom the Caribs came to stay at certain times of the year. If the women had sons, they gave them to the fathers to carry away. Having answered all the questions asked of him, partly by signs and partly by the little the Indians of San Salvador could understand, the Admiral gave him something to eat, gave him some trinkets such as glass beads, and green and red cloth. Then he sent him ashore to get the others to bring gold if they had any.

When the *Niña*'s boat reached shore, the Christians found fifty-five Indians among the trees. They were all naked, with hair as long as the women of Spain wear it, parrot plumes or feathers of other birds tied to the back of their heads, and all of them armed with bows and arrows. The Indian who had been aboard the ship got the others to lay down their bows and arrows and a great club they carry instead of a sword, for they have no iron. When they came to the boat, the Christians stepped ashore and began to trade for bows and arrows as the Admiral had ordered. After they had sold two, the Indians not only refused to sell any more, but did so with scorn. Instead, they ran to where they had left their bows and arrows, with the purpose of getting them and some ropes to tie up our men.

But the Christians were ready for them, and though only seven men in all, they fell on them courageously, cutting one on the buttock with a sword and shooting another in the breast with an arrow. The Indians, terrified by the valor of our men and the wounds our weapons made, fled, most of them leaving their bows and arrows. Many of them would have been killed if the pilot of the caravel, who commanded the boat, had not held back our men.

The Admiral was not at all displeased by this skirmish, thinking these were the Caribs so much dreaded by the other Indians, or at least they were neighbors of the Caribs. From their looks, arms, and actions, these seemed to be a bold and courageous people. He hoped that the islanders, on hearing how seven Christians had behaved themselves against fifty-five fierce Indians, would more respect and honor our men left behind at La Navidad, and would not dare to annoy them. Afterward, about evening, the Indians made a bonfire ashore to show their courage. A boat was sent to see what they wanted, but

they could not be brought to show their faces, so the boat returned.

The bows were made of yew, almost as big as those of France and England; their arrows are made of canes, which are strong and straight, about the length of a man's arm and a half. The arrowhead is made of a small stick hardened in the fire, about twelve inches large and on the end they fix a fish's tooth or bone and put poison on it. The Admiral named this bay, which the Indians called Samaná, Gulf of Arrows. Inland the Christians saw a great deal of fine cotton and chili, the Indians' pepper, which is very hot and has long, partly round fruit. Near land in shallow water there was great abundance of those weeds our men had seen in long strings upon the ocean. They concluded that it grew near land and when ripe broke loose, to be carried out to sea by the current.

XXXI

The Admiral Leaves the Indies Behind and Is Parted from the Pinta in a Great Storm

ON WEDNESDAY, January 16, 1493, the Admiral set sail for Spain from the Gulf of Arrows with a fair wind. Both of the caravels were very leaky and it took much effort to keep them afloat. Cape Santelmo, twenty leagues to the northeast, was the last land they saw. Twenty leagues farther they found all the sea covered with small tunny fish.

On the next two days, January nineteenth and twentieth, they saw many more, and after that, many sea fowl. They found seaweed in strands running east and west with the current, which carried it a great way from land, but not always in the same direction, sometimes moving one way, then another. They saw the seaweed each day until they were almost half way over the ocean.

Holding their course with a fair wind, they made so much way that on the ninth of February the pilots were of the opinion that they were south of the Azores. But the Admiral said they were 150 leagues short, and this was the truth.

As they sailed along with fair weather, the wind began to rise more and more each day, and the sea to run so high, they could scarcely live upon it. For this reason, on Thursday the fourteenth of February, they went whichever way the wind would carry them. The caravel *Pinta,* commanded by Martín Alonso Pinzón, could not stay on course, so ran before the south wind, due north. The Admiral steered northeast to draw nearer to Spain, but the *Pinta* could not follow in the darkness, although the Admiral kept flares burning. When daybreak came, they had lost sight of one another, and each thought the other had gone down.

The Admiral's people gave themselves over to prayers and acts of devotion. They cast lots to see who should go to the shrine of Our Lady of Guadalupe for the whole company, and the lot fell to the Admiral. Afterward they drew for another to go to Our Lady of Loreto, and it fell to a seaman, Pedro de la Villa. Then they cast lots for a third pilgrim to go watch all of one night in the church of Santa Clara de Maguer. The lot fell again to the Admiral. As the storm still increased, they all made a vow to go, barefoot and in their shirts, to the first church of Our Lady they came to, to say their prayers.

Besides these general vows, many made private vows, because the storm now raged so furiously that the Admiral's vessel could scarcely withstand it for lack of ballast, as they had eaten most of their provisions. To make up for this, they now filled all the empty water casks with seawater, which was some help, making the caravel steadier in the water and less likely to capsize.

Of this violent storm, the Admiral says:

I would have been less concerned for the tempest had I alone been in danger, for I know I owe my life to the Supreme Creator, and because I have at other times been so near death. But what grieved and troubled me was the thought that after it had pleased Our Lord to give me faith and certainty to go on this voyage, which had been so successful as to convince my opponents and to make it possible for me to serve Your Majesties with honor and increase to your estate, that now His Divine Majesty should please to prevent all this by my death. And even that would be easier to bear if it were not that the men I had carried with me on promise of happy success would be lost also. They, seeing themselves in that great danger, not only cursed the day they set out but lamented the day my threats and persuasions kept them from turning back as they had often made up their minds to do. But above all, my sorrow was double when I remembered my two sons I had left at school in Córdoba, without friends in a strange country, before I had done, or at least made known to Your Highnesses, some service which might cause you to remember them.

And though on the one hand I comforted myself with the faith that Our Lord would not permit a thing to be left incomplete that was so much for the exaltation of His Church, which I had brought about against so much opposition, yet on the other hand, I thought that He might wish me not to enjoy so much glory in this world because of my demerits.

While caught in this inner confusion, I remembered Your Majesties' good fortune. Even if I were dead and the ship lost, some means might be found so that a conquest so nearly gained might not be lost and that it was possible the success of my voyage should by some means or other come to your knowledge.

For this reason, as briefly as time would permit, I wrote on parchment that I had discovered those lands I promised to. I wrote how many days I had taken and in what direction, the goodness of the lands and the nature of the inhabitants, and how Your Highnesses subjects were left in possession of all I had discovered. I folded and sealed this writing, addressed it to Your Majesties, and on it I promised one thousand ducats to him who would deliver it sealed to you. The purpose of this was that if any foreigner found it, the promised reward might keep him from giving the intelligence to another. Right away I had a great wooden cask brought to me. Having wrapped the parchment in a waxed cloth and put it in a cask, I made the hoops tight and threw it into the sea. The men thought it was some act of devotion. Thinking perhaps it might never be found and as the ship was getting closer to Spain, I placed another cask at the top of the stern-castle, so that if the ship sank, it might float free on the waves.

XXXII

The Admiral Reaches the Azores and His Boat Is Seized

SAILING on in such a great and dangerous storm, on Friday the fifteenth of February, at break of day, one Ruy García, from the roundtop, sighted land, lying to the east-northeast. The pilot and the seamen judged it to be the Rock of Cintra in Portugal, but the Admiral concluded it was one of the Azores. They were no great distance away, but the weather would not let them come to anchor there. Beating about, because the wind was out of the east, they lost sight of the island and discovered another, which they ran about, struggling against a strong cross wind and foul weather, with endless labor in their vain effort to reach land.

The Admiral in his journal says:

On Saturday the sixteenth of February, in the evening, I reached one of those islands at night, but because of bad weather, I could not tell which of them it was. That night I took a little rest, because from Wednesday till then, I had not slept, and was lame in both legs from having been in the open air, wet all the time, and eating little. On Mon-

day morning, having come to anchor, I understood from
some of the inhabitants that it was the island of Santa
Maria, one of the Azores. They all wondered that I had
escaped the fury of the storm, which had held for fifteen
days without letting up.

These people, understanding what the Admiral had discovered, seemed to rejoice, giving praise to God. Three of
them came aboard with some fresh provisions and many
compliments from the governor of the island, who was
away at the town. Here nothing was to be seen but a hermitage, which as they said, was dedicated to the Blessed
Virgin. The Admiral and all his crew remembered the
vow they had made the Thursday before to go barefoot in
their shirts to the first shrine of Our Lady they should
find. They decided they ought to do it here, especially
since it was a place where the people and governor expressed so much affection and tenderness for them. And it
belonged to a king who was a great friend to the sovereigns of Castile.

Therefore, the Admiral asked these three men to go to
the town and get the chaplain, who had the keys to the
hermitage, to come and say a Mass for them there. The
three men agreeing, half the crew went with them, so they
could fulfill their vow, then come back and let the rest go.
They went ashore barefoot and in their shirts as they had
vowed to do. The governor and many people from the
town, who were waiting in ambush, all of a sudden rushed
out upon them and made them prisoners. They also took
their boat, without which the governor thought the Admiral could never escape him.

XXXIII

How the Admiral Weathered Another Storm and Recovered His Boat and Men

THE ADMIRAL thought the men who had gone ashore stayed too long, as they left at daybreak and it was now noon. He feared some misfortune had overtaken them, either on land or on sea. Not being able to see the hermitage from where he lay, the Admiral decided to sail around the point, where the church could be seen. Coming near, he saw many men on horseback, who dismounted and got into a boat to attack the caravel.

The Admiral ordered his men to arm themselves and stand ready, but to make no show of resistance, so the Portuguese might come nearer. When they drew near, their governor stood up, asking a parley, which the Admiral granted, thinking he would come aboard. The Admiral thought he could seize him without breaking his word, since he had seized the Admiral's men without any reason. But the Portuguese did not dare come any nearer than earshot. The Admiral said he was amazed at his irregular way of acting and that none of his men came in the boat, as they had gone ashore with a safe-conduct and offers of help and gifts. The governor himself had sent messages of welcome. The Admiral desired him to consider that besides doing an action which enemies would not be guilty of, and against the laws of honor, the King of Portugal would be mightily offended. The King's subjects were treated with all civility when they landed in the dominions of Their Catholic Majesties, or resided there, without any special safe-conduct just as if they were in Lisbon.

Their Highnesses had given him letters of recommendation to all princes, rulers, and nations of the world, which he would show if the captain drew near. Since such letters were received with respect in all parts, and he and his men were well-treated because of them, they ought to be better treated in Portugal, since their princes were neighbors and kinsmen. Especially he ought to be

well-received as the Catholic Sovereign's Admiral of the Ocean Sea and Viceroy of the Indies he had just discovered, all of which he was ready to show in letters with their royal signatures and seals.

He showed his commissions at that distance and told the governor he might draw near without fear. Because of the peace and friendship between Their Catholic Majesties and the King of Portugal, they had commanded him to treat all the Portuguese ships he met with honor and courtesy. The Admiral added that should the governor obstinately refuse to release his men, it would not keep him from returning to Spain, as he still had enough men to sail to Seville. And once there he would take it on himself to pay him back. Besides that, the King of Portugal would punish him for being the cause of war between him and the Catholic Sovereigns.

The governor and his men answered that they knew neither Their Catholic Majesties nor their letters, nor did they fear them, and they would make him know what a power Portugal was. By this answer, the Admiral suspected there had been some break between the two crowns since he left Spain, and gave him as sharp an answer as his folly deserved. At last, when they were parting, the governor stood up and told the Admiral to bring his caravel to the harbor, for all that he had done was by order of the King his master.

When the Admiral heard this, he asked all on board to bear witness to what the governor said, then called out to the governor and his men, swearing he would not set foot off the caravel until he had depopulated the island and captured two hundred Portuguese to carry home as prisoners. Then he returned to the harbor where he had been,

because the weather would not allow him to do anything
else.

The next day the wind rose, and as the place where he
lay was unsafe, he lost his anchors, and all he could do was
sail for the island of San Miguel. In case he could not
come to anchor there, he made up his mind to ride the
storm out at sea, which was not without much danger, because the sea ran high and he had but three able seamen
and some ship's boys. The rest were landsmen and the Indians, who knew nothing of handling sails and rigging.
But the Admiral himself took the place of the absent. So
the night passed with much toil and danger. When day
came, he noticed that San Miguel was not in sight and the
weather had improved, so he decided to return to the island of Santa Maria to try to recover his men, anchors,
and boat.

He reached Santa Maria on Thursday the twenty-first
of January in the afternoon. Soon after, a boat came off
bearing five men and a notary. After being assured of
their safety, they boarded the caravel, where they spent
the night, as it was late. The next day they said they came
from the governor to know for certain where the ship
came from, and whether it had the King of Spain's commission. Once this was made clear, they would be ready
to show all manner of friendship. They did this now because they could not seize the ship and feared they might
suffer for what they had done.

The Admiral kept his resentment to himself and
thanked them for their courteous offer, and since their
request was in keeping with the martime laws and customs, he was ready to satisfy them. He showed them the
King of Spain's general letter of recommendation, di-

rected to all his subjects and those of other princes, and also his commission for the voyage. When the Portuguese had seen these, they went ashore satisfied, and soon released the seamen and the boat. The men said it was reported on the island that the King of Portugal had sent orders to make the Admiral prisoner by any means possible.

XXXIV

The Admiral Sails from the Azores and Is Forced into Lisbon by a Storm

ON SUNDAY the twenty-fourth of February the Admiral sailed from the island of Santa Maria for Spain. He was in great need of wood and ballast, which he could not take in because of the bad weather, though the wind was fair for his voyage. While they were still one hundred leagues from the nearest land, a swallow alighted on the ship. They supposed it had been driven out to sea, which seemed certain the next day when more swallows and land birds came aboard. They also saw a whale.

On the third of March a tempest arose. After midnight, the sails split. They so feared for their lives that they made a vow to send one man on a pilgrimage to Our Lady of La

Cienta in Huelva, where he was to go barefoot and in his shirt. The lot fell to the Admiral, God showing in this that his offering was more acceptable than that of the others. Besides this, other individual vows were made.

Thus, running on without a rag of sail, nothing but bare masts, with great waves, high winds, and frightful thunder, each of which seemed enough to destroy the caravel, it pleased God to give them sight of land about midnight. But it offered no less danger than the rest, for to avoid being beaten to pieces and running into some place from which they could not get off, they rigged a little sail and rode out the storm till day, when they found they were near the Rock of Cintra, within the boundaries of Portugal.

The Admiral was forced to put in there, to the great astonishment of the people of that country and their seamen, who came running as if to see some wonder, a ship that had escaped so terrible a storm when many had been lost. He came to anchor in the mouth of the river leading to Lisbon on Monday the fourth of March, and sent an express messenger to Their Catholic Majesties with the news of his arrival. He sent another to the King of Portugal, asking permission to go up to anchor off the city, as this place was not safe against anyone who might design to do him harm, pretending it was done by the King's order, to stand in the way of the King of Spain's success.

XXXV

The Admiral's Letter Sent from Lisbon to Luis Santángel and the Spanish Court

SIR:

As I know you will take pleasure in the great victory Our Lord has given me in my voyage, I write this so you will learn how I went over from the Canary Islands to the Indies in thirty-three days with the fleet that the most illustrious King and Queen, our lords, gave me, where I found very many islands inhabited by people without number. I have taken possession of them all for Their Highnesses by proclamation, with royal banner unfurled and no one to gainsay me. To the first island that I found, I gave the name San Salvador, in remembrance of the Divine Majesty who marvelously has given all this. The Indians call it Guanahaní. To the second, I gave the name Santa María de la Concepción, to the third, Fernandina, to the fourth, Isabella, the fifth, Juana [Cuba], and so to each one I gave a new name.

When I reached Juana, I followed the coast to the westward, and found it so large that I thought it must be the mainland, the province of Cathay. And since I found neither towns or villages on the seashore, only small hamlets,

with whose people I could not speak, as they all fled, I
went forward on the same course, thinking I should not
fail to find great cities and towns. At the end of many
leagues, seeing there was no change and the coast carried
me northward, where I did not want to go, as winter was
beginning and I proposed to escape it by going south, I
retraced my course to a harbor I had noticed on the way.
From there I sent two men inland to learn of a king, or
great cities. They travelled three days and found an infin-
ity of small hamlets and countless people, but nothing of
importance. For this reason, they returned.

I understood well enough from other Indians I had already taken that this was an island. Therefore, I followed
the coast eastward for 107 leagues to the point where it
ended. And from there I saw another island to the east at
a distance of eighteen leagues, to which I at once gave the
name Hispaniola. I went there and followed the northern
coast as I had done on Juana. This island and the others
are unbelievably fertile, Hispaniola especially. There are
many harbors on the coast, better than any I know in
Christendom, and many rivers, good and large. Its land
rises from the sea and there are very many sierras and
lofty mountains. All are beautiful, of a thousand shapes,
and all accessible. They are filled with trees of a thousand
kinds, so tall they seem to touch the sky. I am told they
never lose their leaves, which I can understand, as I saw
them as green and beautiful as they are in Spain in May.
Some of them were flowering, some in fruit, and some in
other stages, according to their nature. The nightingale
was singing and other birds of a thousand kinds in the
month of November, when I was there. There are six or
eight kinds of palm, which are wonderful to see, but so

are the other trees, fruits, and plants. There are marvelous pine groves, large open fields, honey, birds of many kinds and a great variety of fruits. Inland there are many mines and people without number. Hispaniola is a marvel.

The sierras and mountains, the plains, fields, and pastures are lovely and rich for planting and sowing, for breeding livestock of all kinds, for building towns and villages. The harbors cannot be believed without seeing them, and so with the rivers, many and great, and good streams, the majority of them bearing gold. There are spices and great mines of gold and other metals.

The people of this island and the others that I have found, both men and women, go naked as their mothers bore them, although some women cover themselves in one place with the leaf of a plant or a net of cotton. They have no iron or steel weapons, nor are they capable of using them. Not because they lack strength, for they are well-built and of handsome stature, but because they are remarkably fearful. They have no other arms than those made from canes cut at seed time, on the end of which they fix a small sharpened stick — and they do not dare to use these. Many times I have sent two or three men ashore to talk to them, and great numbers of people have come out. As soon as they have seen my men nearing, they have fled, even a father not waiting for his son. And this not because harm has been done to anyone. On the contrary, at every point where I have been and been able to talk to them, I have given them all that I had, such as cloth and other things, without getting anything in return. But they are like that, hopelessly timid. It is true that after they have been reassured and have lost their fear, they are so artless and so generous with all they have, that no one would believe it who has not seen it. They never say no when asked for anything they own. On the contrary, they invite everybody to share it, and show enough love to give their very hearts away, and they are content with any trifle given them. I forbade that they should be given things so worthless as pieces of broken crockery and scraps of glass, and ends of straps, although when they got them they thought they had the best jewel in the world. So it was found that a sailor got two and one-half *castellanos* weight of gold for a strap and others much more for other things worth much less. They even took pieces of hoops of wine barrels, and like animals, gave what they had, so that it seemed wrong to me, and I stopped it.

And I gave a thousand good, pleasing things I had brought so they might like us, and more than that, might become Christians and be inclined to the love and service of Their Highnesses and the whole Castilian nation, and strive to help us and give us some of the things they have in abundance and which we need. They do not know any creed nor are they idolaters, only they all believe that power and good are in the sky, and they firmly believe that I, these ships and men, came from the sky. And this does not come from their being ignorant. On the contrary, they have a very keen intelligence. They can navigate all those seas and it is amazing how good an account they give of everything. It is because they have never seen people wearing clothes, or ships like ours.

As soon as I arrived in the Indies, on the first island, I took some of them by force, so that they might learn and give me information about these parts. They soon understood us and we them, either by speech or signs, and they have been very serviceable. I still have them with me and they still think I come from the sky. They were the first to announce this wherever I went, and the others went running from house to house and to the neighboring towns with the loud cries of "Come! Come! See the people from the sky!"

In conclusion, to speak only of that which has been accomplished on this voyage, which was so hasty, Their Highnesses can see that I will give them all the gold they want if Their Highnesses will give me a little help, and I will give them spice and cotton too, as much as Their Highnesses shall command. And I shall find a thousand other things of value, which the men I left behind have found by now.

This is enough. And the eternal God, Our Lord, gives to all those who walk in His way triumph over things which appear impossible, and this was notably one.

So, since Our Redeemer has given this victory to our most illustrious King and Queen, and to their renowned realms, in so great a matter, for this all Christendom ought to take delight and make great feasts, and give solemn thanks to the Holy Trinity for the great exaltation they shall have in turning of so many peoples to our Holy Faith, and afterward for material benefits, for not only Castile, but all Christians will have refreshment and gain from the Indies.

Done in the caravel, off the Azores, on the fifteenth of February, 1493.

At your service,
The Admiral

XXXVI

How the People of Lisbon Flocked to See the Admiral and He Went to Visit the King

ON TUESDAY the fifth of March, the master of the great guard ship [Bartholomew Dias, discoverer of the Cape of Good Hope] that lay in the harbor came with a boat full of armed men to the Admiral's caravel, asking him to come along and give an account of himself to the King's officers, as was the practice of all ships coming into the harbor. The Admiral answered that the King of Spain's admirals did not have to obey such summonses, nor might they leave their ships to give an account of themselves to anyone, on pain of death, and he was resolved to do his duty.

The master asked him to send his boatswain, at least.

The Admiral said it was all one to him, he would not send even a ship's boy.

The master, seeing the spirit and good sense of what the Admiral said, asked him to prove he sailed in the name of the Catholic Sovereigns by showing their letter — that might satisfy his captain.

This was but reasonable, so the Admiral showed him

the Catholic Sovereigns' letter, with which he was satisfied.

The master went back to his ship to tell the captain what had happened, and he came immediately in great state, with trumpets, fifes, and drums, offering the Admiral his congratulations and his services.

The next day, it being known in Lisbon that the ship came from the Indies, so many people went aboard to see the Indians and hear the news that the caravel could not hold all of them, and the water was covered with boats. Some of the Portuguese praised God for so great a victory, but others raged that they had lost the discovery because of their King's skepticism and indifference. So the day was spent midst throngs of people.

The next day the King ordered his officers to present the Admiral with all sorts of refreshments and all things he stood in need of for himself or his men, at the King's expense. At the same time, he wrote to the Admiral, congratulating him on his safe arrival, and desiring, since he was in his kingdom, that he would come to see him.

The Admiral had misgivings about going, but as the King was at peace with Their Catholic Majesties and had treated him courteously, and to remove any suspicion that he came from the lands the Portuguese were conquering, he consented to go to Valparaiso, nine leagues from Lisbon, where the King was in residence.

He arrived on Saturday night the ninth of March. The King ordered all the nobles of his court to go out to meet him. When he came into the King's presence, the King did him great honor, commanding him to keep his cap on and be seated. The King heard the particulars of the successful voyage with a cheerful countenance, then offered

him all he stood in need of for the service of Their Catholic Majesties, although he thought that by the treaty he had with Their Majesties the discoveries belonged to him.

The Admiral answered that he knew nothing of that treaty, but that he had carefully observed his orders, which were not to go to the Portuguese possessions of Mina or Guinea.

The King said all was well, and everything could be worked out peaceably and justly.

After they had spent a long time in this sort of conversation, the King commanded the Prior of Crato, the most important man among them, to entertain the Admiral and show him every courtesy and favor, which was done. Having stayed there all Sunday and until after dinner on Monday, the Admiral took leave of the King.

On his way to Lisbon, he passed a monastery where the Queen of Portugal was staying. She sent word that he must not leave without calling on her. She was much pleased to see him, and did him all the favor and honor that was due the greatest lord. That night a gentleman came from the King to let the Admiral know that if he pleased to go by land to Spain he would go with him, provide lodgings and necessities as far as the borders of Portugal.

XXXVII

The Admiral's Triumphant Return to Spain

AT TWO in the afternoon on Wednesday March thirteenth, the Admiral set sail for Seville, and on Friday following at noon, put in the Saltés and anchored in the harbor of Palos, where he had set out on the third of August, 1492, seven months and eleven days earlier. He was received by all the people in a procession, giving thanks to God for his success, which, it was hoped, would spread the Christian religion and add to the dominions of the Catholic Sovereigns. The people of that place looked on it as a great matter that he set out from there and most of the men with him were native to it, though many of them, through Martín Alonso Pinzón's fault, had been mutinous and disobedient.

It happened that when the Admiral came to Palos, Pinzón had reached Galicia, and planned to go by himself to Barcelona, to carry the news to Their Catholic Majesties. But they sent him orders not to come without the Admiral, with whom he had sailed on that voyage of discovery. At this Pinzón was so annoyed and offended that he went home quite sick and died of grief within a few days.

Before Pinzón reached Palos, the Admiral set out over-

land for Seville, meaning to go from there to Barcelona, where the Catholic Sovereigns were staying. He was forced to spend some time on the way because of the great admiration of the people wherever he went. They ran from all the neighboring towns down to the road to see him, the Indians, and the other things he brought.

Continuing on his way, he got to Barcelona about the middle of April, having before sent to Their Highnesses an account of the happy outcome of his voyage, which was pleasing to them. They ordered a most solemn reception, as befitting a man who had done them such a singular service. All the Court and the city went out to meet him, and Their Catholic Majesties sat in public with great state, on rich chairs under a canopy of cloth of gold. When he went to kiss their hands, they stood up for him as for a great lord. They would not let him kiss their hands, but had him sit down beside them. After he gave a brief account of his voyage, they gave him leave to retire to his apartment, where he went, accompanied by the whole Court. He was so highly honored and favored by Their Highnesses that when the King rode about Barcelona, the Admiral was on one side of him and the Infante Fortuna on the other. Before this none went by the King's side but the Infante, who was his near kinsman.

XXXVIII

The Admiral Sails Again for the Indies

THE CATHOLIC Sovereigns confirmed all they had granted the Admiral before:

Ferdinand and Isabella, by the grace of God King and Queen of Castile, León, Aragón, Sicily, Toledo, Valencia, Galicia, Majorca, Minorca, Seville, Sardinia, Jaen, and so forth: Forasmuch as you, Christopher Columbus, are going by our command, with some of our vessels and men to discover and subdue some islands and mainland in the Ocean Sea, and it is hoped that by God's help some of the islands and mainland in the ocean will be discovered and conquered by your means and conduct; therefore, it is just and reasonable, that since you expose yourself to such danger to serve us, you should be rewarded for it. And we being willing to honor and favor you, our will is that you, Christopher Columbus, after discovering the said islands and mainland shall be our admiral of them, viceroy and governor, and that for the future you may call and style yourself, Don Christopher Columbus, and that your sons and successors may call themselves dons, admirals, viceroys, and governors of them.

Orders were given at Barcelona, carefully drawn up, for the Admiral's return to Hispaniola, to relieve the men left there, to enlarge the colony and conquer the rest of the island, as well as any others that might be discovered.

All things necessary for settling those countries being provided, the Admiral left Barcelona for Seville in June. There he diligently began to fit out the fleet Their Catholic Majesties had ordered him to. In a short time seventeen ships, great and small, were made ready, well stored with provisions, and with all things thought necessary for peopling of those countries, including handicraftsmen of all sorts, laborers, and farmers. The fame of gold and other wonders of the land drew so many gentlemen and others persons of rank that it was necessary to reduce the number. Fifteen hundred men went aboard in all, and some took horses, donkeys, and other beasts, which were afterward of great use in the settlement of Hispaniola.

On Wednesday, September 25, 1493, having completed all preparations, the Admiral weighed anchor in the harbor of Cadiz, while my brother and I looked on, and stood southwest for the Canary Islands.

A Word About the Text

THE TEXT in this book is taken from the first English translation of Ferdinand Columbus's *Historie,* made in the eighteenth century for Churchill's *Voyages.* That translation is based on an Italian translation of the original Spanish, which has been lost. The present version adds no fictions and puts no words into the mouth of Ferdinand; he wrote everything that appears here other than the direct words of his father, although some of the sentences in the old English translation have been made clearer and more direct and some passages that modern scholarship finds unreliable have been left out. The text has been tightened to make the essential narrative move more quickly. Ferdinand's historical account has always been the most complete and reliable source for material on Columbus the man and on the discovery, making allowances where necessary for the natural pride of a son.

The Admiral's letter to Luis Santángel is not included in Ferdinand's *Historie;* it has been added here at the appropriate moment in the narrative. The text of the letter is based on *Select Letters of Christopher Columbus,* translated and edited by R. H. Major, London, 1870, some of which has been retranslated from the original Spanish at a level of greater simplicity and directness by the present editors.

Acknowledgments

Acknowledgment is made to:

The scholarship of Samuel Eliot Morison.

The scholarship of Benjamin Keen.

Glossary of Special Words and Measures

caravel — A sailing vessel somewhat smaller than a *nao* or ship; the *Santa María* was a ship, the *Niña* and *Pinta* were caravels.

castellano — A gold coin worth about five dollars in American money today.

Castile — An honored part of Spain used to stand figuratively for all Spain.

dates — Columbus used Old Style dates, ten days behind the modern calendar.

ducat — A gold coin worth about three dollars in American money today.

escudo — A gold coin used to replace the ducat, of comparable value.

league — A distance of 3.18 nautical miles.

maravedí — A coin worth a little more than a penny in American money.

sterncastle — A castle-like structure at the rear of a ship, originally used as a tower to fight off attackers.

Index